MISSION POSSIBLE
BIBLE STUDY

MISSION POSSIBLE BIBLE STUDY

Go Create a Life That Counts

Tim Tebow
with A. J. Gregory

WATERBROOK

LIBRARY OF CONGRESS CATALOGING-IN-PUBLICATION DATA

Names: Tebow, Tim, author. | Gregory, A. J., author.
Title: Mission possible Bible study / Tim Tebow with A. J. Gregory.
Description: First edition | [Colorado Springs, Colorado] : WaterBrook, an imprint of Random House, a division of Penguin Random House LLC, 2022.
Identifiers: LCCN 2021030971 | ISBN 9780593194034 (paperback) | ISBN 9780593194041 (ebook)
Subjects: LCSH: Self-actualization (Psychology)—Religious aspects—Christianity—Textbooks | Vocation—Christianity—Textbooks.
Classification: LCC BV4598.2 .T433 2022 | DDC 248.4—dc23
LC record available at https://lccn.loc.gov/2021030971

Printed in the United States of America on acid-free paper

waterbrookmultnomah.com

2 4 6 8 9 7 5 3 1

First Edition

Interior book design by Virginia Norey

SPECIAL SALES Most WaterBrook books are available at special quantity discounts when purchased in bulk by corporations, organizations, and special-interest groups. Custom imprinting or excerpting can also be done to fit special needs. For information, please email specialmarketscms@penguinrandomhouse.com.

Contents

Welcome

Welcome to the *Mission Possible Bible Study!* I'm so glad you're here. We're going to dive into a topic that I'm sure you've had a ton of conversations about with your friends and maybe even strangers: *purpose*. I hear all kinds of people, young and older, ask the very same question: "What is my purpose in life?"

It's a weighty inquiry. And it doesn't have a one-size-fits-all answer. Our purposes are as unique as we are, and they can ebb and flow in different seasons of life. So, rather than try to answer that question specifically and permanently for you, I want us to explore further what it means to live a life on mission. When we ask about "purpose," what we're really asking is how we find significance. We are given one life. How do we make it count?

Most of us want each of our days on this earth to matter. We want our lives to count for something greater than just existing. We want to believe that something more is going on here than simply feeling temporary pleasure or accumulating compliments, degrees, or social status. As followers of Jesus Christ, living lives of purpose is mission possible because of what God has done for us through Jesus.

Purpose flows from God's ultimate mission to redeem His people. This is foundational. Without Christ, life will eventually feel relatively meaningless (no matter how carefully we attempt to curate experiences, relationships, and events). Only through new life in Him are we able to enjoy a relationship with God and glorify Him with our lives. We can also play a part in His grand purpose by loving and serving others, using the unique gifts, talents, and skills that

God has given to each of us with the intention of making Him known to those around us.

Be honest with yourself:

- Do you want your life to have a deeper sense of meaning?
- Do you want a greater sense of purpose intertwined in your day?
- Do you want to do things, starting now, that will leave a mark on this world for Jesus?

I promise you, God's Word shows us that these things are mission possible for each and every one of us.

Let's get started and find out how!

How to Use This Guide

You can work through this Bible study in a group setting or on your own. Also, it's formatted to work in conjunction with my book *Mission Possible* and the video teaching. If you haven't read the book or won't get a chance to watch the video segments, don't worry. There's plenty of content that will help you begin—today—to activate growth in your life.

This Bible study is divided into six sessions that each include the following:

1. Mission Vision
2. A Quick Look in the Rearview Mirror (sessions 2–6)
3. Jump Start
4. Talk About It
5. Video Teaching
6. Mission-Driven Discussion
7. Send-Off and Group Prayer
8. Your Midweek Mission: Four Days of Exercises and Prayer to Go Deeper

If you want to maximize your experience outside your small group, spend time in the personal study portion at the end of each session. This includes four days of assignments to reflect on what you've learned and what God has been speaking to you about.

What You'll Need

Unless otherwise marked, all the Scripture references in this guide are offered in the New American Standard Bible (NASB). If you prefer a different version, have a Bible or Bible app handy to look up the verses in the translation of your choice. Space for writing is provided in this guide, but feel free to use a journal or digital device to jot down notes or anything that speaks to you. Finally, you'll get the most out of this guide if you read it alongside my book *Mission Possible*.

MISSION PURPOSE

Mission Vision

Couple the *why* and the *how* in your life to execute the good works that God has already prepared you to do. Your mission is possible because of what Jesus has already done for you.

Jump Start

Purpose is a word that is often thrown around in Christian circles and can mean many things. But our greatest purpose is to glorify God. Our purpose is also felt in our everyday lives.

How do we know we have purpose?

Simple: God tells us!

We are His workmanship, created in Christ Jesus for good works, which God prepared beforehand so that we would walk in them. (Ephesians 2:10)

If you're wondering what those "good works" might be, let me ask you a question: For what circumstances have you ever been in a place where God was leading you to see someone hurting or in need and you felt driven to help? The answer to this question could be a pointer to your starting place.

There is a fundamental principle, a *conviction*, that you must cling to in order to fulfill the good works God has called you to do. You must first understand that you were created perfectly in love, by love, and for love, and part of that creation package includes an amazing plan and purpose. When you acknowledge this truth, God will supply the power and vision you need to live a mission-possible life.

You are not an accident. You are not a mistake. God molded you into a one-of-a-kind masterpiece. You are one of one. When you arrive at that critical juncture of acceptance and surrender, you will be able to wholeheartedly ask God to use you for His purpose no matter what your strengths or weaknesses are.

Even though we're called to a mission, that mission is not about us. There are certain things that can happen only through His power and His power alone. You can be the most eloquent speaker or have the most entertaining presence or most impressive scholarly credentials, but there are opportunities and hearts that only God can ordain and open.

When we live mission possible, fully trusting in God's power and doing our part, we can fulfill our purpose every day, even in the middle of difficult circumstances or suffering or when a phone call brings devastating news. When life is chaotic or we're stuck in a season of waiting, our mission doesn't stop. We may be reminded of the lack of control we have over circumstances, but even in hardship, we're awakened to the truth that we can bring light into darkness. We can look for ways to be compassionate and take action. We put the interests of others ahead of our own. When we feel overcome by challenging circumstances, we should refuse to be overcome by evil; rather, we must overcome evil with good (see Romans 12:21).

Talk About It

When you hear the word *purpose*, what comes to mind?

Video Teaching

Watch video session 1. While viewing the video, use the outline and space below to record key ideas or any thoughts you want to remember.

➢ _____

_____

➢ _____

_____

➢ _____

_____

➢ _____

_____

➢ _____

_____

➢ _____

_____

➢ _____

_____

Mission-Driven Discussion

1. In the video teaching, I talked about how we all have a mission in life! A definition for *mission* is a task or job someone is given to do. How have you experienced a sense of mission in the past?

_____

_____

_____

_____

2. In the video teaching, I also shared that a mission-possible life starts by knowing the person of God. As we explored Mark 4:35-41, we saw the disciples ask the Great Question, "Who, then, is this?" We all must give an answer to who we say Jesus is. In your current stage of life, how would you answer the Great Question? Who is Jesus to you?

_____

_____

_____

_____

3. As I mentioned above, *purpose* is a word that is often thrown around in Christian circles but is rarely defined. Simply put, *purpose* is the reason why something is created, used, or exists. Think about the things you interact with every day. What things, objects, or people have purpose in your life and why?

_____

_____

_____

_____

4. What are some things in your life that have prevented you from doing what you may have sensed God calling you to do? Looking back, what would you have done differently?

_____

_____

_____

_____

5. "Your purpose in life is not just about you." This statement can be easy to give lip service to but is tough to live. Where in your life does your pursuit of purpose need to grow in the investments you're making in others?

_____

_____

_____

_____

6. Read the following words spoken by Jesus and recorded in Scripture:

Even the Son of Man did not come to be served, but to serve, and to give His life as a ransom for many. (Mark 10:45)

I have not come to call the righteous to repentance, but sinners. (Luke 5:32)

The Son of Man has come to seek and to save that which was lost. (Luke 19:10)

I did not come to judge the world, but to save the world. (John 12:47)

What was Jesus's ultimate purpose?

_____

_____

_____

_____

7. Read from *Mission Possible,* page 35:

I love how [Paul] launched the fourth chapter [of Philippians]: "Rejoice in the Lord always; again I will say, rejoice!" (verse 4). The word *rejoice* isn't one I use often in my vernacular. I doubt you do either. When's the last time you said to a friend, "What a beautiful day! Let's rejoice together!"? Never, right? While spending time in my NIV study Bible, I came across a footnote that made more sense to me. It substituted "expressing confidence in" for "rejoice in." Expressing confidence made a lot of sense to me.

While imprisoned and facing the possibility of being killed for his faith at any moment, Paul could have written about how anxious, worried, and afraid he was. Instead, he chose to record an expression of his unshakable confidence in God, which he wanted other believers to share in.

In a time of fear and panic, I want to be someone who expresses confidence in God. I also want this to be true when life doesn't seem seamless. I need to be confident in God when I'm launching a mission that I'm certain I can't fulfill in my own power. I want to express confidence in God when uncertainty holds me in its grip. I want to express confidence in God when I'm tired because every little thing that can go wrong does. I want to express confidence in God's plan for me when I feel overwhelmed with the details and lose sight of the vision.

What are two ways that you can express confidence in God, thereby experiencing joy in Him, while living a mission-possible life?

Send-Off and Group Prayer

It's clear that God has a purpose for our lives both as a community and as individuals and that in and through any circumstance, we can live with a mission-possible focus. This hope is evidenced not through our capabilities or our experience but through the power of the living God activated within our hearts.

Let's give it to God in prayer:

- Thank God for giving us His one and only Son to die for us in the greatest rescue mission of all time.
- Ask Him to reveal opportunities in which you can shine for Him.
- Pray for an unshakable confidence to know that God has a special plan and purpose for your life.
- Ask Him for the courage to step out in obedience when you feel His calling to give, serve, love, or sacrifice but are hesitant to lean in.
- Ask your Father in heaven to use even your most trying seasons to bring faith, hope, and love to those needing a brighter day.

Your Midweek Mission:
Four Days of Exercises and Prayer to Go Deeper

Day 1 Study and Reflect

Read Ephesians 2:1–10:

> You were dead in your offenses and sins, in which you previously walked according to the course of this world, according to the prince of the power of the air, of the spirit that is now working in the sons of disobedience. Among

them we too all previously lived in the lusts of our flesh, indulging the desires of the flesh and of the mind, and were by nature children of wrath, just as the rest. But God, being rich in mercy, because of His great love with which He loved us, even when we were dead in our wrongdoings, made us alive together with Christ (by grace you have been saved), and raised us up with Him, and seated us with Him in the heavenly places in Christ Jesus, so that in the ages to come He might show the boundless riches of His grace in kindness toward us in Christ Jesus. For by grace you have been saved through faith; and this is not of yourselves, it is the gift of God; not a result of works, so that no one may boast. For we are His workmanship, created in Christ Jesus for good works, which God prepared beforehand so that we would walk in them.

In two or three sentences, summarize the main ideas of the above passage.

_____

_____

_____

_____

Did you notice that you were once spiritually "dead" in your sin but God made you alive and free in Jesus Christ? This is not by your own doing. God accomplished this without your help; therefore, you can take no credit for your salvation. It is by faith alone in Christ that God now considers you a marvelous work of art.

In Ephesians 2:10, Paul wrote, "We are God's *masterpiece*. He has created us anew in Christ Jesus, so we can do the good things he planned for us long ago" (NLT). This verse eloquently details *who* you are in Christ: God's masterpiece. Other translations use the terms *handiwork* (NIV), *workmanship* (ESV), and *creative work* (NET).

What comes to mind when you think about a masterpiece?

_____

_____

_____

_____

The Greek word Paul uses here for *masterpiece* is *poiēma* (poy'-ay-mah), which means "something made" or "a work; creation," referring specifically to something God has made.[1] It is used only one other time in Scripture, referencing God's creation as evidence to His existence (see Romans 1:20). The making of humanity in Genesis 1:26–27 was God's first masterpiece, but because our sin tainted that work, He has gifted us with a new divine act of creation through His Son.

Read the following passages. Jot down what you observe about your *new* self in Christ.

If anyone is in Christ, this person is a new creation; the old things passed away; behold, new things have come. (2 Corinthians 5:17)

Put on the new self, which in the likeness of God has been created in righteousness and holiness of the truth. (Ephesians 4:24)

_____

_____

_____

_____

Because you are God's workmanship, there is nothing boring, bland, or insignificant about you. Being a child of God is the result of unparalleled artistic skill. What's interesting is that *poiēma* is where we derive our English word *poem* from. Paul was saying, "You are divine poetry."

Though mankind is not a piece of writing, we are a master work in which our human makeup was carefully (and specifically) chosen to reflect the image of the Most High, and we were designed to live in a consistent rhythmic relationship with our Creator. As we breathe in life, truth, and love, we exhale, exerting energy and focus for His glory—a pattern of intimate repetition.

What currently hinders you from seeing yourself as God's masterpiece?

_____

_____

_____

_____

In the New Living Translation, the second half of Ephesians 2:10 says, "He has created us anew in Christ Jesus, so we can do the good things he planned for us long ago," referring to our having been saved by grace through faith (see verse 8). Verse 10 in the New American Standard Bible reads, "We are His workmanship, created in Christ Jesus for good works, which God prepared beforehand so that *we would walk in them.*"

There is a phrase in sports that broadcasters and journalists use to describe athletes who perform at the highest levels: "poetry in motion." Athletes such as Michael Jordan, Tiger Woods, and Muhammad Ali have been called this because of their graceful movements on the court, on the green, and in the ring, respectively. The phrase may be a cliché, but it's a good one! To be poetry in motion represents the height of tactful skill, sensitivity, and competitive elegance.

As God's poem, we, too, are set in motion. However, it's not us performing; it's the Spirit of God working in and through us. As God's image bearers and recipients of His grace, we faithfully move in preordained acts of love for the sake of Christ. God did not design us to be static. All Christians are God's poetry in motion.

being created in God's image + redemption through Christ + living in His good works = God's masterpiece

Meditate on and memorize Ephesians 2:10 (translation of your choice). How does this verse better help you understand the character of God and who you are because of Him?

_____

_____

_____

_____

Day 2 Review, Reflect, and Remember

Review chapters 1 and 2 in *Mission Possible*.

Reflect: Write down what you learned, a breakthrough you experienced, or a shift in perspective you gained from this lesson, the book, the video, or discussions. Prepare to share with the group next week.

_____

_____

_____

_____

What scripture spoke to you most this week? Try to memorize it. Write it down and then put it someplace where you'll see it when you spend some time alone each day; for example, on the bathroom mirror, your car dashboard, or your laptop cover.

_____

_____

_____

_____

Remember: From *Mission Possible,* page 12:

A mission-possible life has less to do with us and more to do with others. Mission living means being motivated by something other than yourself. It's scary. It's also pretty exciting. It can be unpredictable (but in a good way). It will also require submitting your preferences to God, and sometimes that doesn't feel very good or doesn't make you look as favorable as you'd like. That is where trusting God becomes crucial. If you've made the decision to trust Him,

He gives you the mission and makes it possible. Trust that He's got better plans for your life than you do.

Day 3 Study and Reflect

The only way to experience the active power of God in our lives is to be filled with the Holy Spirit. What—or rather, *who*—is the Holy Spirit?

The Holy Spirit is a distinct person of the *Trinity*, a word describing the unity of God as one in essence and three in persons (God the Father, God the Son, and God the Holy Spirit). The *HarperCollins Bible Dictionary* notes that the Holy Spirit is "the mysterious power or presence of God that operates within individuals and communities, inspiring or empowering them with qualities they would not otherwise possess. The term 'spirit' translates Hebrew *ruakh* and Greek *pneuma*, words denoting 'wind,' 'breath,' and, by extension, a life-giving element. With the adjective 'holy,' the reference is to the divine spirit, i.e., the Spirit of God."[2]

Throughout the Scriptures, God's Spirit empowers and transforms God's people to live righteously and minister to others in order to fulfill His purposes. Identified in various ways, God's Spirit is referred to as *Spirit, Holy Spirit, Spirit of God, Spirit of the Lord, Holy Ghost,* and *Helper.* In the Old Testament, the Holy Spirit is mentioned in broad strokes:

- through the acts of the creation of the world (see Genesis 1:2)
- delivering the nation of Israel out of Egyptian slavery (see Exodus 15; Isaiah 63:11–12)
- empowering Israel's leaders (kings, prophets, judges) (see Judges 3:9; 1 Samuel 10:6; 2 Peter 1:21)
- ultimately, developing a moral code for God's people

In the New Testament, the Holy Spirit is spoken of in specific detail. As promised by Christ in John 14:16–17, the Spirit of God was sent on the Day of Pentecost (see Acts 2:1–4) as a Helper (Greek *Paraklētos*) for

His followers. This is one of my favorite attributes of God. I want a Helper. I need a Helper with my frustration, with my thoughts, and with my bitterness. I need Someone I can cast my burdens upon.

Paraklētos—also called *Comforter, Advocate,* or *Intercessor*—means "one called alongside to help."[3] The book of Acts demonstrates the Spirit's supernatural role in the spread of the gospel and growth of the church throughout the Mediterranean area. The same power that was on display in the first century is still working in the lives of believers today. So, what exactly does the Holy Spirit do?

The Holy Spirit indwells, intercedes, fills, speaks, instructs, convicts, gives spiritual gifts, reminds, leads, strengthens, reveals, acts, restrains, facilitates, and works powerfully in the salvation and maturing of every Christian.

In Ephesians 5:17–21, Paul wrote,

Do not be foolish, but understand what the will of the Lord is. And do not get drunk with wine, in which there is debauchery, but be filled with the Spirit, speaking to one another in psalms and hymns and spiritual songs, singing and making melody with your hearts to the Lord; always giving thanks for all things in the name of our Lord Jesus Christ to our God and Father; and subject yourselves to one another in the fear of Christ.

In context, Paul contrasted getting drunk on wine with the filling of the Spirit. Here the idea is that we should not be controlled by outside influences; rather, we should submit to and obey God. Submission to God produces human flourishing.

Author and Bible commentator Max Anders noted,

Ephesus was a center of pagan worship and ritual. The Ephesian culture worshiped Baccus, the god of wine and drunken orgies. They believed that to commune with their god and to be led by him, they had to be drunk. . . . Paul was talking about how to commune with the God of heaven, how to live for him, how to serve and obey him, how to determine his will. It was natural for him to draw the contrast between how the god of Ephesus is served and how the God of heaven is served. With the God of heaven, you do not get drunk with wine. Rather, you are filled with the Spirit.[4]

As believers, the Spirit never leaves us, but when we are disobedient, our sinful behavior can limit the active work of God in our lives. On the other hand, when we obey God's commands—His will—we can expect to see the Spirit's fruit in our lives.

In summary, at the moment of salvation, we are indwelled by the Holy Spirit. When we submit to God, we are filled with the Holy Spirit. This is an ongoing work as we humble ourselves before God.

What role has the Holy Spirit played in your life? What have you been taught about Him up to this point? How has He helped you?

_____

_____

_____

_____

Read the following verses:

I will ask the Father, and He will give you another Helper, so that He may be with you forever. (John 14:16)

In Him, you also, after listening to the message of truth, the gospel of your salvation—having also believed, you were sealed in Him with the Holy Spirit of the promise. (Ephesians 1:13)

[God] also sealed us and gave us the Spirit in our hearts as a pledge. (2 Corinthians 1:22)

According to those verses, how necessary is it for the Holy Spirit to be active in your life?

_____

_____

_____

_____

Write down your experiences of how the Holy Spirit has convicted or prompted you in some way. What was the outcome? How can you be more open to listening to the Holy Spirit going forward?

_____

_____

_____

_____

In what area of your life do you believe the Holy Spirit needs to be more in control?

_____

_____

_____

_____

Day 4 Remember and Read

Remember: From *Mission Possible,* page 28:

God has a habit of making His presence known or inter-vening in impossible missions. It seems as if He's drawn to predicaments for which no plan B or Z exists. If it can't be done in the natural, if it can't be figured out by the efforts of humans alone, if it's a problem without a solution, it's the perfect venue for God to do His best work.

The anchor of the gospel rests in the truth that we can-not save ourselves by our pedigrees, good works, or impres-sive career histories. We receive the free gift of salvation through what Jesus has done for us on the cross. This is one of the reasons the Son of God said, "The things that are impossible with people are possible with God" (Luke 18:27).

When we make the decision to trust Him with our lives, we are automatically seated at the table of the humanly im-possible. It's not about what we can do; it's about what God can do through us.

If you are following along in the *Mission Possible* book, read chap-ters 3 and 4 this week. Capture any statements or phrases that moti-vated or challenged you that you'd like to share with the group next week.

_____

_____

_____

_____

A Prayer for You

Heavenly Father, I pray for the person holding this book right now. I thank You for creating them with a purpose and a plan. Remind them that because of what You did on the cross, they are more than enough. They are counted as righteous. They are more than a conqueror. Give them the courage, the determination, and the perseverance to focus on loving You and others and bringing Your light into a world of darkness. In Jesus's name I pray. Amen.

Session 2

USE WHAT YOU HAVE WHERE YOU ARE

Mission Vision

Whatever you find yourself doing—whether you're on your knees in prayer, using your hands to search for a clean diaper, or with your head buried in a table full of books—do it wholeheartedly, with purpose and intention.

A Quick Look in the Rearview Mirror

Share one thing that stood out to you most from last week's lesson, video, reading, or discussion.

Jump Start

Ecclesiastes is a tough Bible book to digest, at least on the surface. Take, for instance, how the writer front-loaded this ancient text:

> *"Futility of futilities," says the Preacher,*
> *"Futility of futilities! All is futility." (1:2)*

Other translations use the more familiar refrain "vanity of vanities" (ESV). Some offer the phrase "Everything is meaningless" (NIV). The English word *vanity* in this verse translates into the Hebrew word *hebel*, which means "vapor."[5] Life is but a vapor, a breath, here one moment, gone the next. And much of it passes without our grasping a firm handle on its meaning. If you continue reading Ecclesiastes, you can see that it's not much like a Hallmark movie. It does, however, prepare you for real life. Not only does it unveil that as life cycles through its time, difficulty will sprout along the way, but it also shares that life itself is difficult. It's a heavy book weighted with dark shadows. But wait, that's not all. Ecclesiastes also offers great wisdom. It reminds us to enjoy life. Just as there is a time to mourn, there's also a time to laugh. In particular, I love what it says in chapter 9, verse 10: "Whatever your hand finds to do, do it with all your might."

Sure, life may be ripe with twists and turns and more questions than answers, but that doesn't mean our role on this earth is to curl up in the fetal position and hide in a corner until Jesus comes back. We must do our part, whatever it is God has us doing in the moment we are in, to the best of our ability.

Read verse 10 again. Note, it doesn't say to do your best at what you want to do or to do your best at the things that you are really good at. The teaching is, whatever you are doing, do it well. This applies to parenting, studying, leading, serving, cleaning—pretty much anything you can think of that you do on a daily basis.

There are always opportunities to live a mission-possible life. You don't have to fly to a foreign country to have impact for Jesus. I encourage you to start this week by simply finding a way to kindly help someone around you. It doesn't have to be huge. Just step out of your comfort zone and find a way to make an extra effort to let others know that they matter. Show them that they are loved.

There are so many ways to do this: say a prayer for someone as you fold laundry; ask a team member how he or she is doing and really mean it; do the work that is set before you with excellence, without complaint; shine the light of Christ wherever you are. It's not about the size of the gesture; it's about the size of the heart behind it. God doesn't care about what you have to offer; He is more interested in your willingness. As long as you are willing to be open to His opportunities, His prompting, and His leading, He can use you to make a positive difference wherever you are. God has planted in you special gifts and abilities that only you can offer the world.

Never forget that in whatever you do, your main audience is God, not others. That's why the apostle Paul reminds us to put our whole hearts into everything we do and with God's purposes in mind. We're called to live life for His glory, as Colossians 3:23 explains: "Whatever you do, do your work heartily, as for the Lord and not for people."

Talk About It

How is purpose interwoven in everyday life, particularly in the moments you would label as ordinary?

Video Teaching

Watch video session 2. While viewing the video, use the outline and space below to record key ideas or any thoughts you want to remember.

➢ _____

_____

➢ _____

_____

➢ _____

➤ _____

_____

➤ _____

_____

➤ _____

_____

➤ _____

_____

Mission-Driven Discussion

1. In the video teaching, I discussed that a critical part of living a mission-possible life is trusting the plan of God. You may not always like where you're at or the situation you're in, but God has you there for a reason. Identify a job or task you don't necessarily enjoy and explain why you don't like it.

_____

_____

_____

_____

2. In the video teaching, I also shared, "I don't believe the mission starts with your job or being qualified. I believe the mission starts with your heart." Part of trusting the plan of God is transcending whatever we do, wherever we are. How can you give God glory in and through the situation you wrote about in question 1?

_____

_____

_____

_____

3. There can be a stark contrast between the hopeful awe we assume a life lived for God entails—mountaintop experiences, tangible evidence of His presence, immediate fruit from our human efforts—and the ordinariness of daily life, which often scatters that sacred space and steals the anticipated wonder. Talk about a time when you felt the ordinary overwhelm the mission you believed God was calling you to.

_____

_____

_____

_____

4. In *Mission Possible*, I talk about my elementary school choir teacher, Miss Nancy, and the effect she had on my life. This mission-driven leader viewed her job not just as a means to get a paycheck but as a channel to change lives. From *Mission Possible*, pages 40–41:

> I may have been basically taking up space in choir due to my lack of talent, but I was happy to do my best for this special teacher. Miss Nancy had a gift. More than one, actually. But it wasn't just that she was a great teacher who had remarkable music talent. She was passionate about her position. She used what she was doing and where she was planted to make a difference. Miss Nancy cared about the students. And she made every one of us feel special, even the kids who couldn't carry a tune past the first three notes. Like me.
>
> What I especially loved about her was how she flipped what I had considered awful into something fun. It wasn't her skill that made this happen; it was the place in her heart she taught from. Miss Nancy's spirit was steeped in joy, from the smile that always glowed on her face, to her positive attitude, to her words of encouragement to all students— the ones who had talent and the ones who were better at other things. Even the teachers who worked with her, like Miss Tammy, shared her passion. Let me be clear that my dislike of choir and singing didn't change. If I could sing, I would have loved it, but I sucked. It was my admiration for Miss Nancy and her team that made me want to do more than just stand there and mouth some lyrics. My teacher created an environment that grew musical gifts and drew out the best in her students. It's what I saw her do with excellence, and it's what made me consider her one of my favorites.

Talk about someone in your life, past or present, who made a positive impression on your life because he or she genuinely cared for you and invested in your well-being and success as an individual. How has that influenced you?

_____

_____

_____

_____

5. Read 1 Corinthians 3:9: "We are God's fellow workers; you are God's field, God's building." The New International Version puts it like this: "We are co-workers in God's service." Whether paid or unpaid, recognized or overlooked, behind a desk or on a field, we are partakers of a divine nature. How does this verse revitalize your outlook on everyday living?

_____

_____

_____

_____

6. Name a crisis, tragedy, or hardship you experienced that God used for a greater purpose (for example, to build your character or encourage someone else). Not everything has a neat and tidy ending, but sometimes we get to see some of the positive outcomes of difficulty.

_____

_____

_____

_____

7. If you truly believe that God has created each of us with unique gifts and abilities and that we each have unique experiences for unique purposes, how does that change how you view your worth and the worth of others?

_____

_____

_____

_____

8. In Psalm 136 of the New Living Translation, "his faithful love endures forever" is repeated _twenty-six_ times! When you feel worn out, exhausted, defeated, and unworthy, and are questioning whether or not you can continue to live mission possible, how does this phrase bring peace and comfort?

_____

_____

_____

_____

Send-Off and Group Prayer

Today we have learned that a mission-possible life is one that's lived twenty-four hours of every day. This doesn't mean you'll never get a chance to sleep or watch a movie; it means that every moment can bring purpose, even the ones in which we rest and recharge. It's possible to cultivate purpose in every season and to drive the mission of the gospel forward no matter where you are planted and what you have to offer.

Let's close this session in prayer:

- Thank God that His presence is found in every day and in everything you do.
- Ask Him for an awareness of His purpose in the activities and responsibilities that make up each day.
- Ask your Father in heaven for opportunities to love and serve others and use the experiences you have been through to bring others closer to Him.
- Ask God to help you become aware of and release the distractions that keep you away from His purpose for your life.

Your Midweek Mission:
Four Days of Exercises and Prayer to Go Deeper

Day 1 Study and Reflect

Over the past thirteen years, the Marvel Cinematic Universe (MCU) has created a superhero frenzy across the globe. With twenty-four movies (and counting), the MCU's box office total stands at $8.5 billion domestically and a whopping $22.5 billion worldwide, making it the most profitable movie franchise of all time.[6] Outside the fact that the Russo brothers are two incredibly talented producers and screenwriters, one of the reasons Marvel movies have captivated audiences is that mankind is fascinated with supernatural powers. Whether it's Captain America's remarkable strength and stamina or Bruce Banner's uncontrollable anger or Peter Parker's Spidey sense, we all are innately drawn to figures who have special abilities and use them to protect the weak and fight for good.

All superheroes have particular abilities that help them withstand challenges and overcome obstacles. These superpowers set them apart from mere mortals, as well as enemies. As Christians, we, too, possess special powers. Spoiler alert: they may not be what you think. As mentioned in session 1, when you make a decision to trust Jesus Christ as Lord, the Holy Spirit comes to live inside you. And as promised by Jesus in Luke 24:49 and assured in Acts 1:8, when the Holy Spirit comes upon us, we receive power.

When you think of God-given "superpowers," what comes to mind?

_____

_____

_____

_____

The heart is central to who we are as human beings and distinguishes us as creatures made in the image of God. It is with our hearts that we can praise and worship our God. But it is only through the transformation of the heart that we can experience an intimate, personal relationship with God Himself. The Bible tells us that when we make the decision to trust in Jesus, God gives us a new heart.

In Ezekiel 36:26–27, the word of the Lord came to the prophet, saying, "I will give you a new heart and put a new spirit within you; and I will remove the heart of stone from your flesh and give you a heart of flesh. And I will put My Spirit within you and bring it about that you walk in My statutes, and are careful and follow My ordinances."

Of all the Holy Spirit superpowers, the power to be transformed in the likeness of Jesus is perhaps the greatest. It is the source and the lifeblood of who we are becoming. Though our hearts were once hard like stone, in Christ, through the power of the Holy Spirit, we become new creations. The Spirit's power changes our hearts from being sin focused to being God focused.

What were you like before you put your faith in Jesus? What changes have you seen since you received a new heart?

_____

_____

_____

_____

When I talk about Holy Spirit superpowers, what I mean is the Spirit of God activated in us. Read 1 Corinthians 12:1–11. Paul talks about special gifts, or abilities, that God through His Spirit gives to each of us.

Concerning spiritual gifts, brothers and sisters, I do not want you to be unaware. You know that when you were pagans, you were led astray to the mute idols, however you were led. Therefore I make known to you that no one speaking by the Spirit of God says, "Jesus is accursed"; and no one can say, "Jesus is Lord," except by the Holy Spirit.

Now there are varieties of gifts, but the same Spirit. And there are varieties of ministries, and the same Lord. There are varieties of effects, but the same God who works all things in all persons. But to each one is given the manifestation of the Spirit for the common good. For to one is given the word of wisdom through the Spirit, and to another the word of knowledge according to the same Spirit; to another faith by the same Spirit, and to another gifts of healing by the one Spirit, and to another the effecting of miracles, and to another prophecy, and to another the distinguishing of spirits, to another various kinds of tongues, and to another the interpretation of tongues. But one and the same Spirit works all these things, distributing to each one individually just as He wills.

Name some of these superpowers that the Holy Spirit gives.

_____

_____

_____

_____

What gifts do you think you possess? How can you use these gifts to build up others?

_____

_____

_____

_____

Day 2 Review, Reflect, and Remember

Review chapters 3 and 4 in *Mission Possible*.

Reflect: Write down what you learned, a breakthrough you experienced, or a shift in perspective you gained from this lesson, the book, the video, or discussions. Prepare to share with the group next week.

_____

_____

_____

_____

What scripture spoke to you most this week? Try to memorize it. Write it down and then put it someplace where you'll see it when you spend some time alone each day; for example, on the bathroom mirror, your car dashboard, or your laptop cover.

_____

_____

_____

_____

Remember: From *Mission Possible*, pages 37–38:

Being a mission-possible Christian has less to do with holding a religious vocation and more to do with developing an intimate relationship with Jesus. Mission stems from embracing our identity in Him. When we deepen our walk with Jesus, He invades every part of our lives. He doesn't become real only at a church service, small-group meeting, or worship event. We are image bearers of God on the field, in the boardroom, and in our kitchens. Each minute. Each day. Every day.

Whatever you are tasked with in the everyday—even what you believe is the most trivial of duties or responsibilities, or a boring job you are always complaining about—find a way to invite purpose into that space. What can you do to make someone's life better after he or she has interacted with you? How can you approach a challenge you've been avoiding knowing God is on your side? If you're changing diapers or teaching kindergarten in a virtual setting or folding sweatshirts in retail, think about what you could be doing differently or doing more of (or less of) that unveils whose you are. When you begin to live beyond the surface of what you see, you begin to transcend the ordinary.

Day 3 Study and Reflect

One of my good friends I've learned much from (and continue to) is Pastor Louie Giglio. His church, Passion City, hosts annual Passion Conferences, for which I've had the opportunity to speak a few times over the years. *Passion*. Isn't that a great word to use for the name of a conference? The interesting thing about that word is how it's been misused over the years. Today it often refers to the idea of romance or an athlete's raw emotion. However, when you investigate the word's origin, you find something different. The word *passion* was first introduced in the thirteenth century. It comes from the Latin root word *pati*, which means "to suffer."[7] This Latin word was used to describe Christ's *passion*—His physical suffering on the cross. In the Greek, we see the same thing. The root verb for passion, *paschō*, means "to be afflicted" or "to undergo sufferings,"[8] in either a good or bad sense. Passion moves and motivates, but there's a cost. At its core, true biblical passion is one's willingness to suffer!

If you didn't have this historical context, how would you have described the meaning of the word *passion*?

_____

_____

_____

_____

In taking on a new (but old) meaning, think about the things you're willing to suffer for. What do you desire so deeply that you're willing to endure pain for it? Saying it another way, if pain gets in the way of goals you are desperate to achieve, are you willing to go through it?

_____

_____

_____

_____

If you already know where your passion lives, you probably have at least a glimpse of what a mission-driven life looks like. If you're reading this and thinking, *Whoa, passion is intense. I'm not sure what my "passion" is,* that's okay. Use the questions above to start thinking in a way that should direct your every step, choice, and decision in life.

Another word that relates to the idea of passion is *compassion.* I'm sure you can probably now guess it's original definition—and it's not what *Merriam-Webster* defines it as. *Compassion* means "to suffer with one another."[9]

Throughout the Gospels, Jesus was often moved with compassion. Here are several examples:

When Jesus heard about John, He withdrew from there in a boat to a secluded place by Himself; and when the people heard about this, they followed Him on foot from the cities. When He came ashore, He saw a large crowd, and felt compassion for them and healed their sick. (Matthew 14:13–14)

When Jesus went ashore, He saw a large crowd, and He felt compassion for them because they were like sheep without a shepherd; and He began to teach them many things. (Mark 6:34)

As He approached the gate of the city, a dead man was being carried out, the only son of his mother, and she was a widow; and a sizeable crowd from the city was with her. When the Lord saw her, He felt compassion for her and said to her, "Do not go on weeping." And He came up and touched the coffin; and the bearers came to a halt. And He said, "Young man, I say to you, arise!" And the dead man sat up and began to speak. And Jesus gave him back to his mother. (Luke 7:12–15)

What do you notice about these passages? Are there any similarities? How does Jesus show compassion?

_____

_____

_____

_____

When Jesus came to earth, He was willing to suffer—not only *for* us but *with* us. Hebrews 4:15 says, "We do not have a high priest who cannot sympathize with our weaknesses, but One who has been tempted in all things just as we are, yet without sin." Jesus is our model for both passion and compassion. You have the ability to suffer for and suffer with, just like Christ. He was tempted and tried, just like you and me. Many times, we don't find our deepest calling or purpose without suffering along the way.

What are two ways you can live with passion this week and show compassion to others?

_____

_____

_____

_____

Day 4 Remember and Read

Remember: From *Mission Possible,* page 62:

When you get tired, true passion is what will see you through. When no one is around to help boost your confidence, passion will help you take the next step. When you get stuck or hit a wall, passion will give you momentum to recover and press forward. In your desire to live armed with purpose, find out where your passions lie. What are you willing to sacrifice for? What are you willing to pursue or stand up or fight for in the face of challenge and adversity?

As you follow along in the *Mission Possible* book, read chapter 5 this week. Make sure you jot down or highlight any statements or phrases that motivated or challenged you that you'd like to share with the group next week.

_____

_____

_____

_____

A Prayer for You

Father, thank You that You have placed a special purpose and plan in the heart of this reader. I pray they offer You their willingness to use their time, their resources, their experiences, and whatever they have in this season of life to make a difference for You. Equip them with what they need to live a mission-possible life. Remind them of the power of the Holy Spirit that lives within them. In Jesus's name I pray. Amen.

THROUGH
A GLASS DARKLY

Mission Vision

The Bible tells us that our steps are ordered by the Lord (see Psalm 37:23). It doesn't tell us that He will unveil every step of the way before we set out.

A Quick Look in the Rearview Mirror

Share one thing that stood out to you most from last week's lesson, video, reading, or discussion.

Jump Start

People often think that once you follow the Lord, decisions become easy. The path on which God has designed for you to walk becomes perfectly clear—free of debris, weeds, and muck—and that you've been warned well ahead of time of any twists and turns that lie around the next bend. I think most of us understand that this utopian scenario is about as real as filter-free photos on social media. I can't speak on behalf of Christians everywhere, but I will say that if you're in a place of uncertainty, anchored to the unknown at a cross-roads or even in a wide open space, you're not alone. You're also not a terrible Christian.

I've experienced many challenges in which I felt completely stuck. *Do I pursue the call I feel pressing on my heart? But what is it exactly that I do next anyway? Do I commit to mission X or mission Y?* Many times, I've prayed and have asked the Lord to show me the answers. I've sought wise counsel. I've fasted. I've searched through the Bible. And each time I was faced with a challenge, despite my best efforts to seek a concrete answer of what to do or the next step to take, I heard . . . nothing.

What I've realized is that just because you don't think you've heard an answer doesn't mean God isn't leading you, and it doesn't mean He isn't with you. It's important to walk by faith. One of the best ways to find the right next step is through obedience to what God has put right in front of you.

Here are a few questions I often ask myself when I need clarity on where to step out in faith:

- How is God calling me to step out *today*?
- Who has He placed in my path to love?
- Where has He asked me to make a difference?

As unsure about the details as you may be, as unqualified as you may feel, as stuck as you may seem without having a perfect plan in place, do it anyway. Your obedience expresses the nature of your heart and your willingness to trust God.

So say yes to His call on your next step.

Donate your time, talent, resources, and abilities to bring light into a world of darkness. Your yes, your obedience in the direction of where God is calling you right now, might change a life or even the world. And both matter dearly!

God has an awesome plan for you. You might not see what He is doing. You might not know how He is working. But when you step out and show a little courage, demonstrate a little boldness, you are going to be amazed with what He can do with your life. It doesn't mean the path is going to be easy, but it is going to be worth it.

Talk About It

Talk about the last time you had to deal with uncertainty.

Video Teaching

Watch video session 3. While viewing the video, use the outline and spaces below to record key ideas or any thoughts you want to remember.

➢ _____

_____

➢ _____

_____

➢ _____

_____

➢ _____

_____

➢ _____

_____

➤ _____

_____

Mission-Driven Discussion

1. In the video teaching, we talked about the reality of not getting life's full picture. We don't always know what God is up to, and we must make peace with this fact. Give an example of how you have experienced this truth in your life. Is there anything you're currently questioning?

_____

_____

_____

_____

2. In the video teaching, I say, "Even though you can't see the full picture, you get to know the Person that does, you get to walk with the Person that does, you get to trust the Person that does." This person is Jesus. How has He given you confidence and hope in the midst of the unknowns?

_____

_____

_____

_____

3. How often do you struggle with worry? In what ways do you try to trust God rather than allow doubt and the pressures of uncertainty to dampen your faith?

_____

_____

_____

_____

4. Name an instance in which you were forced to do away with your plan B (or C or Z) and take a leap of faith, believing that God would provide and come through for you? How has that experience strengthened your faith?

_____

_____

_____

_____

5. From *Mission Possible,* pages 78–79:

It's not about knowing every detail or having an answer for every question; it's about accepting the mission God has prompted in your heart and following it, one step at a time. . . .
    You move forward in your mission even if you make a mistake or take a wrong turn. . . .

We are responsible for keeping it moving, even if it's taking us longer than expected, even when our friends think we're crazy, and even if others question our motives. When you don't know what to do, depend on God. You don't need it all figured out. You just need Him to know it. And He does it. The Bible tells us, "Oh, the depth of the riches, both of the wisdom and knowledge of God! How unsearchable are His judgments and unfathomable His ways! For who has known the mind of the LORD, or who became His counselor?" (Romans 11:33–34). We can't figure God out. And you know what? I don't want to serve a God I can figure out. If we could, we'd hang right on His level, and if we did that, we wouldn't need Him at all. God has the details figured out. He knows the twists and turns that are coming, as well as the opportunities and provision. Rest in this and find peace that His knowledge is greater than ours.

How does the truth that God is God and you are not encourage you?

_____

_____

_____

_____

6. Read 2 Timothy 2:13:

If we are faithless, He remains faithful, for He cannot deny Himself.

Is there a relief that comes in knowing that God will continue to be faithful despite your questions and doubts? Have you ever felt this type of relief or comfort?

_____

_____

_____

_____

7. Name a time when you couldn't make a decision and prayed for God to show you a sign to help you in the process. What was the outcome? What did you learn through that experience?

_____

_____

_____

_____

Send-Off and Group Prayer

Today we have learned that success is not about knowing every detail of God's plan for our lives. It's about following His plan. It's about being obedient. It's about being willing to say, "You know what, God? I don't know what Your plan is, but whatever it is, I'm open to it and I will do it. Whatever You want me to do, that's what I want to do."

Let's close this time together in prayer. Here are some ideas from this session that can guide your conversation with God:

- Thank Him for walking with you every step of your life.
- Ask Him to help you trust in Him and not lean on your own understanding.
- Surrender any doubt or worry that you have struggled with in allowing God to lead you.
- Thank Him for His faithfulness, His great love, and His guiding presence, which will be with you for eternity.

Your Midweek Mission:
Four Days of Exercises and Prayer to Go Deeper

Day 1 Study and Reflect

First Corinthians 13 is one of the most commonly known passages in the Bible. If you've read it before or been to a wedding recently, you're probably aware that it's often referred to as the "love" chapter. However, toward the end of the passage, Paul made a seemingly unusual statement:

> Now we see in a mirror dimly, but then face to face; now I know in part, but then I will know fully, just as I also have been fully known. (verse 12)

What is Paul talking about? At first glance, this verse can be a mouthful. But with context, it sheds light on how we can trust God with limited knowledge this side of heaven.

The phrase "Now we see in a mirror dimly" has been translated differently over the years. Originally, it was first rendered in the 1560 Geneva Bible as "Now we see through a glass darkly." Though it doesn't appear in many modern translations, "through a glass darkly" has become a popular title for a variety of novels, biographies, poems, plays, and movies.

The Greek word for mirror, or glass, in this passage is *esoptron*— meaning an object for looking into.[10] According to most scholars, glass mirrors were probably introduced around the first century and were typically made of polished brass, bronze, or other metals. In the *1 Corinthians* Tyndale New Testament Commentary, Dr. Leon Morris noted that the city of Corinth was famous for its mirrors but that few Christians would have had the financial means to afford one of good quality. Therefore, due to the low quality, the "reflection as in a mirror" would be distorted.[11]

Paul was using an analogy here. Because ancient handheld mirrors reflected a warped or partial image, he compared this idea to our partial or limited knowledge of life and God. Essentially, Paul was saying we can see the world only through an incomplete or imperfect lens. First Corinthians 13:12 reminds us that we cannot see the full picture.

However, even though there isn't perfect knowledge, there is real hope. The picture of God became most clear in the person of Jesus Christ. Knowing Jesus allows us to "know in part." Receiving spiritual gifts also allows us to "know [God] in part." But, ultimately, until Christ returns and you see Him "face to face," your understanding will be bent.

The reality is that, as Christians, we must live with some level of uncertainty. We don't see it all, but we trust a God who does and loves us through it all. He doesn't know what you'll be doing only next year; He knows all things for all time—past, present, and future. It's not about what we know that provides our security; it's who we know.

Read Romans 11:33:

> Oh, the depth of the riches, both of the wisdom and knowledge of God! How unsearchable are His judgments and unfathomable His ways!

Paraphrase that verse in your own words.

_____

_____

_____

_____

Read Psalm 139:1–6:

LORD, _You have searched me and known me._
You know when I sit down and when I get up;
You understand my thought from far away.
You scrutinize my path and my lying down,
And are acquainted with all my ways.
Even before there is a word on my tongue,
Behold, LORD, _You know it all._
You have encircled me behind and in front,
And placed Your hand upon me.
Such knowledge is too wonderful for me;
It is too high, I cannot comprehend it.

What does this passage tell you about God's perfect knowledge?
How does the extent of His knowledge make you feel about Him?
About yourself?

_____

_____

_____

_____

Which of the statements in the psalm do you find most comforting? Why?

_____

_____

_____

_____

Read Matthew 10:29–31: "Are not two sparrows sold for a penny? Yet not one of them will fall to the ground outside your Father's care. And even the very hairs of your head are all numbered. So don't be afraid; you are worth more than many sparrows" (NIV).

What does this passage tell you about the value God puts on your life? How will knowing this truth affect your daily life?

_____

_____

_____

_____

Day 2 Review, Reflect, and Remember

Review chapter 5 in *Mission Possible*.

Reflect: Write down what you learned, a breakthrough you experienced, or a shift in perspective you gained from this lesson, the book, the video, or discussions. Prepare to share with the group next week.

_____

_____

_____

_____

What scripture spoke to you most this week? Try to memorize it. Write it down and then put it someplace where you'll see it when you spend some time alone each day; for example, on the bathroom mirror, your car dashboard, or your laptop cover.

_____

_____

_____

_____

Remember: From *Mission Possible,* page 86:

You don't know what God has in store for you when you step out and walk by faith. One idea or one thought that propels you into action, such as dropping off a Bible to someone in need or lavishing love and joy onto people who are normally looked at as though they don't belong, can change the course of their days, and even their lives. One step forward in a mission-possible life can unveil to you the glory of God you may never have experienced before.

Day 3 Study and Reflect

In 2 Corinthians 5:7, Paul instructed believers to "walk by faith, not by sight." You may be familiar with this verse, perhaps having seen it used as an Instagram caption or on a coffee cup.

What initially comes to mind when you hear that phrase?

_____

_____

_____

_____

Second Corinthians 5:7 contains two elements: posture and contrast. Paul first instructs Christians to walk. The Greek word for walk is *peripateō*, meaning to conduct oneself, behave, live. It's used in a metaphorical sense to denote a lifestyle.[12] As Christians, our posture, the way we live, should be guided by our faith in God and not by what is necessarily seen in this present world.

Paul then contrasts walking by faith with walking by sight. He emphasized that these two principles should never mix—hence "*not* by sight." The Greek word for faith is *pistis*. It is a word that evokes trust and persuasion. The Greek word for sight is *eidos*. This refers to outward appearance, what is physically seen.[13] Therefore, based on this meaning, to walk by faith means to live in confidence despite the unknown, and to walk by sight is to live by only what is visibly understood—which is not always a good way to live.

Read verses 6–9:

Being always of good courage, and knowing that while we are at home in the body we are absent from the Lord—for we walk by faith, not by sight—but we are of good courage and prefer rather to be absent from the body and to be at home with the Lord. Therefore we also have as our ambition, whether at home or absent, to be pleasing to Him.

In context, Paul was discussing our future after death. As Christians, our earthly bodies as we experience them are only our temporary homes. Our destination is in heaven with Christ, awaiting our final resurrection one day into God's renewed and perfect creation. Though we cannot see or experience heaven prior to our death, Paul is confident in the fact that there is a place for us in glory with God. Therefore, no matter what we face this side of death, we should make it our goal to trust and please Him in everything we do, in anticipation of going "home."

What are some areas in which you struggle with faith and sight?

_____

_____

_____

_____

To walk by faith is relatively countercultural in our modern world today. We live in a society where we demand proof to determine what is true. That isn't all bad, but many people tend to assume that the Christian faith is a blind faith—that there is no evidence or logical reason for belief. So, is Paul suggesting we walk by this type of faith? No.

Read Hebrews 11:1:

Faith is the certainty of things hoped for, a proof of things not seen.

How does the author of Hebrews define faith?

_____

_____

_____

_____

As the New International Version says, "Faith is confidence in what we hope for and assurance about what we do not see." Faith is confidence and assurance. This confidence and assurance that Paul is talking about comes from what Christ did on the cross. In his first letter to the church in Corinth, Paul proclaimed that the Resurrection is essential, the core doctrine, to the gospel:

> I handed down to you as of first importance what I also received, that Christ died for our sins according to the Scriptures, and that He was buried, and that He was raised on the third day according to the Scriptures, and that He appeared to Cephas, then to the twelve. After that He appeared to more than five hundred brothers and sisters at one time, most of whom remain until now, but some have fallen asleep; then He appeared to James, then to all the apostles; and last of all, as to one untimely born, He appeared to me also. . . . And if Christ has not been raised, then our preaching is in vain, your faith also is in vain. (1 Corinthians 15:3–8, 14)

Don't miss what Paul is saying here. The resurrection of Jesus Christ is the cornerstone of our faith. Without Jesus being raised from the dead, our faith is in vain. If He did not come back to life, defeating sin and death, He would be just like every other man: dead, gone, and forgotten. But He did! Jesus conquered the grave and appeared to more than five hundred eyewitnesses (see verse 6). To walk by faith is to trust in the same God who walked this earth and made dead men come alive, who performed miraculous signs healing hundreds, who turned water into wine, who preached repentance and not religion, and who ultimately sacrificed Himself so that we may be assured of our new home in heaven. The Christian faith is not a blind faith. It is defined by conviction based on facts.

Think about a time when you walked by sight, or feelings, rather than by faith. What was the outcome? What did the Lord teach you through this experience?

_____

_____

_____

_____

Day 4 Remember and Read

Remember: From *Mission Possible,* page 92:

We are called to love God and to love people. The best definition of the verb form of *love* that I know is to choose the best interest of another person over your own and act on his or her behalf. Let's find people who are in need and act on their behalf.

When you are willing to be used by God, He will open your eyes to opportunities to step in and fill a gap. It's okay to feel afraid or have questions while taking the first step. Do it anyway. Just keep moving the ball five yards. And five more yards. And five more.

Once you spark movement, it always leads to another opportunity, and another, and another after that. But it always starts with one step.

As you follow along in the *Mission Possible* book, read chapters 6 and 7 this week. Capture any statements or phrases that motivated or challenged you that you'd like to share with the group next week.

_____

_____

_____

_____

A Prayer for You

Lord God, I lift up the reader of this Bible study before You. Thank You for ordering their steps. Steady their ways according to the promises found in Your Word. May they seek You with all their heart and find assurance in Your faithfulness rather than answers to every question. Remind them You are leading them on this journey and that You will never leave them or forsake them. In Jesus's name I pray. Amen.

Session 4

PUSH THROUGH
THE RESISTANCE

Mission Vision

When we live mission possible, we don't back down from discomfort, adversity, or resistance. We push through with the end goal in sight.

A Quick Look in the Rearview Mirror

Share one thing that stood out to you most from last week's lesson, video, reading, or discussion.

Jump Start

Living mission possible doesn't mean that each step forward is going to add up to a perfect journey. It means you simply take one step in front of the other. Left. Right. Repeat. When you begin to realize you are living not for selfish gain but for a bigger purpose—to further the kingdom, to love and serve God and others—your perspective begins to change. You understand the importance and even necessity of sacrificing what you want right now for what you want most later in life. Short-term sacrifice produces long-term gain.

In order for significance to define your life, you have to be willing to do things that may not be popular or fun all the time. You have to make the hard choices and do the hard things. Living a mission-possible life means fighting through not just unmet preferences, what you want and when you want it, but also adversity. It's easy to get hyped and motivated when you first feel inspired to make a difference for Jesus, but what happens when you get kicked in the face? Or cut? Or knocked down? What happens when the plans you crafted fail or the momentum you have built slows down and you feel absolutely tired or defeated?

These may not be the most enjoyable of times, but these are moments when your convictions will surpass the temporary and when your purpose will transcend hardship. When you choose *not* to sacrifice, *not* to get back up, or *not* to push through the resistance, you end up missing out. You end up losing depth in your relationships and not realizing the true meaning of passion or the depth of your potential. You become unable to experience the depth of provision and purpose that God extends to each of us, and you don't give Him the chance to come through in all the ways He would like.

I always want to make the most of what God has given me. I want to be a good steward of my time, my talent, my treasure, and my abilities, even during the times that seem terrible. I have a feeling the same is true for you. If you don't make sacrifices and tackle the adversity that comes, one day you will end up looking back and asking yourself questions like these:

Who could I have become?

What could I have accomplished?

How much impact could I have made?

What legacy could I have left?

Making sacrifices and pressing through the hard times isn't easy, but when you truly want to live mission possible, in faith you will do what you need to do in order to reach through the resistance.

Talk About It

What happens to your faith when you are in situations that stress or stretch you?

Video Teaching

Watch video session 4. While viewing the video, use the outline and spaces below to record key ideas or any thoughts you want to remember.

➢ _____

_____

➢ _____

_____

➢ _____

_____

➢ _____

_____

➢ _____

_____

➢ _____

_____

➤ _____

_____

Mission-Driven Discussion

1. In the video teaching, I mentioned how people will often ask me, "Timmy, how do I know my purpose or calling?" I typically respond back with a question: "Has God ever pricked your heart or opened your eyes to a problem, to a people group, to someone hurting, to someone or something in need?" I ask this because I don't know each person's specific, individual calling and purpose in life, but I do believe God convicts us to act on His behalf for people. How would you answer that question? Has God pricked your heart or opened your eyes for something or someone? If so, for whom or for what?

_____

_____

_____

_____

2. In the video teaching, I shared that when we're trying to live out our purpose, at some point there will be resistance—from friends, family, teachers, coaches, coworkers, your boss, random people on social media, and so on. Describe how you have experienced resistance in your spiritual journey.

_____

_____

_____

_____

3. What is the connection between the Christian faith and the cost of discipleship?

_____

_____

_____

_____

4. Read Romans 12:1–2:

I urge you, brothers and sisters, by the mercies of God, to present your bodies as a living and holy sacrifice, acceptable to God, which is your spiritual service of worship. And do not be conformed to this world, but be transformed by the renewing of your mind, so that you may prove what the will of God is, that which is good and acceptable and perfect.

Paul describes our bodies as living sacrifices. What does this look like in practice?

_____

_____

_____

_____

5. From *Mission Possible,* page 97:

A life of significance is steeped in sacrifice. The Salazars were willing to sacrifice their material possessions, even necessities like a car, for a mission they believed in. It got uncomfortable for them. But that's what happens when we sacrifice. The balance is much lower than what makes us feel secure. The work seems overwhelming, and the time is never enough. But when we live mission possible and put the needs of others before ourselves, we are invited to see not what is *us* possible but what is only *God* possible.

What sacrifices have you made as your spiritual service of worship?

_____

_____

_____

_____

What sacrifices do you wish you would have made?

_____

_____

_____

_____

What sacrifices do you want to make now?

_____

_____

_____

_____

6. A relationship with God is based not on feelings but on faith, yet we are human beings who experience the reality of being swept up in emotions. Some of them are more difficult to handle than others, particularly if we find ourselves struggling in a rough season of life. Talk about which emotions are the hardest for you to deal with and why.

_____

_____

_____

_____

7. Name one way you can trust God more than the negative emotions that overwhelm you.

_____

_____

_____

_____

Send-Off and Group Prayer

In this session, we learned that challenges and sacrifice are part of being a Christian. In life, we either are about to go into a tough season, are on our way out of one, or are in the middle of that hard place. And although God never promised us an easy journey, He did promise that we can do all things through Christ who strengthens us (see Philippians 4:13).

Let's close in prayer. Here are some ideas from this session that can guide your conversation with God:

- Thank Him for His strength and power in helping you embrace resistance and learn from it.
- Ask Him to show you areas in which you can be more open to sacrificing your material needs for His greater glory.
- Ask God to remind you that what you go through on earth is temporary and help you focus on the things that are eternal.
- Thank Him that there is always a purpose in the midst of perseverance.

Your Midweek Mission:
Four Days of Exercises and Prayer to Go Deeper

Day 1 Study and Reflect

In one of Jesus's final conversations with His disciples, He told them that upon His departure, trouble and suffering would be coming. In John 15:20, He said, "Remember the word that I said to you: 'A servant is not greater than his master.' If they persecuted me, they will also persecute you" (ESV). For a Christ follower, resistance is inevitable. Jesus promised that there will be obstacles in our lives that seem to hinder our progress. But when we live mission forward, we don't shy away from these obstacles; we move forward with the end goal in sight.

Think of a time when you encountered resistance. What did it look like? How did you feel? How did you respond?

_____

_____

_____

_____

Throughout the book of Acts, there are numerous examples of embracing resistance. But there is one account in particular that sets a precedent for Christian living.

Not long after Jesus ascended to heaven, thousands of people in Jerusalem chose to trust Christ as their Messiah and Savior. As the early church began to grow, so did the needs of the people. In order to assist and provide for all the widows, the twelve disciples summoned the new church community and instructed the people to select seven men among them (see Acts 6:3).

These men weren't just any men. To be part of this elite care team, a man was required to be "full of the Spirit and of wisdom." The purpose of this group was to help serve widows in need while the Twelve continued to pray and preach God's Word in the city. Among the seven selected was a man named Stephen:

> The announcement found approval with the whole congregation; and they chose Stephen, a man full of faith and of the Holy Spirit, and Philip, Prochorus, Nicanor, Timon, Parmenas, and Nicolas, a proselyte from Antioch. . . . And Stephen, full of grace and power, was performing great wonders and signs among the people. (verses 5, 8)

How does the Bible describe Stephen? Why do you think the people selected him?

_____

_____

_____

_____

The Bible says that Stephen not only was elected as a leader to serve but sometimes went to the synagogue to talk with Jewish people about God. In one specific instance, Stephen encountered resistance like no other Christian before him.

Read Acts 6:8–7:60. As you read Stephen's story, document the specific opposition he faced in each of the following verses:

Verse in Acts	Resistance Stephen Faced
6:9	
6:11	
6:12	Stephen was arrested.
6:13	
7:54	
7:57	
7:58	

Notice Stephen's attitude toward those who were persecuting him (see 7:59–60). What did he ask the Lord to do? Why do you think he asked that?

_____

_____

_____

_____

Stephen ultimately died for his faith, becoming the first Christian martyr (see verse 60). He experienced harsh disagreement, charges of false testimony, being innocently convicted, and eventually being killed in an inhumane way. But when faced with resistance, Stephen embraced it for the sake of the gospel. When asked if the false witnesses were telling the truth, instead of saying no, Stephen took the opportunity to boldly teach on Israel's history, revealing God's redemptive plan and pointing out the Jewish council's stubbornness in rejecting and murdering Jesus. Stephen knew what was at stake—his life—but he had his eyes on the prize (literally): eternity with Jesus.

Read these passages and paraphrase each of them in the space provided.

Matthew 5:11–12

_____

_____

_____

_____

1 Peter 4:12–14

_____

_____

_____

_____

What do these passages have in common, and how do they build confidence in mission-possible living?

_____

_____

_____

_____

Day 2 Review, Reflect, and Remember

Review chapters 6 and 7 in *Mission Possible.*

Reflect: Write down what you learned, a breakthrough you experienced, or a shift in perspective you gained from this lesson, the book, the video, or discussions. Prepare to share with the group next week.

_____

_____

_____

_____

What scripture spoke to you most this week? Try to memorize it. Write it down and then put it someplace where you'll see it when you spend some time alone each day; for example, on the bathroom mirror, your car dashboard, or your laptop cover.

_____

_____

_____

_____

Remember: From *Mission Possible,* pages 105–106:

> When our foundation chooses employees, one of the es-
> sentials we look for is whether they have had to deal with
> strong resistance or hardship in the execution of their
> missions. Same with our business partnerships. We want
> to understand if and how they endured something tough.
> Did they stay the course? Did they remain faithful? Did
> the opposition make them better, create more wisdom in
> them, or prepare them for the next battle? We want to
> partner with people who have faced strong resistance and
> experienced growth through it. It's one of the most tell-
> ing attributes of what relationships will thrive in the long
> term.

Day 3 Study and Reflect

The Christian life is built on sacrifice. It begins with the sacrifice God
made in sending His only Son to die for humanity.

In your own words, jot down the meaning of *sacrifice.*

_____

_____

_____

_____

Sacrifice is typically not the most pleasing word in our vocabulary.
For many of us, it often brings to mind feelings of loss, pain, and
hurt. It expresses the idea of giving something up that is valuable in
order to help another person. However, in its Latin origin, the word

sacrifice means "to make sacred or holy,"[14] usually referring to the priestly act of offering something to God.

Throughout the Old Testament, we read about sacrificial offerings made on behalf of God's people. These sacrifices were of two kinds: unbloody (such as firstfruits and tithes, meat and drink offerings, and incense) and bloody (burnt offerings, peace offerings, sin-and-trespass offerings). These sacrifices were meant to secure forgiveness of sin and satisfy God's righteous demand of judgment.

In the greatest example of sacrifice, God gave up what was most precious to Him: His Son. He did this in order to restore the broken relationship between humanity and Himself. John 3:16–17 says, "God so loved the world, that He gave His only Son, so that everyone who believes in Him will not perish, but have eternal life. For God did not send the Son into the world to judge the world, but so that the world might be saved through Him."

How does this popular verse give more clarity about the heart of God?

_____

_____

_____

_____

As a result of the Fall (see Genesis 3), the Levitical sacrificial system was established and provided temporary reconciliation. Sacrifices were to be made every year, over and over again. This was exhausting for the Jewish people. In order to provide a simple (but not easy), long-term, eternal solution for mankind, God sent His Son to be a sacrifice on our behalf. In Philippians 2:6–8, Paul wrote,

[Christ Jesus, who] already existed in the form of God, did not consider equality with God something to be grasped, but emptied Himself by taking the form of a bond-servant and being born in the likeness of men. And being found in appearance as a man, He humbled Himself by becoming obedient to the point of death: death on a cross.

According to this passage, not only did God the Father sacrifice His Son, but God the Son, Jesus Christ, sacrificed the privileges of heaven to take on human form and live in obedience to the Father's will. Think about that. The God of this universe loves you so much that He stripped Himself of the glory He had in heaven to walk on this earth and be your Savior. He did this in order to make you holy. In understanding Old Testament sacrifices, God flipped the script when He sent His Son. Instead of you making sacrifices to God, He made a sacrifice for you.

Think about a time when you knew that God was asking you to give up something significant for the benefit of someone else. Describe the effect your sacrifice had on others.

_____

_____

_____

_____

Ephesians 5:1–2 tells us, "Be imitators of God, as beloved children; and walk in love, just as Christ also loved you and gave Himself up for us, an offering and a sacrifice to God as a fragrant aroma." God set the standard, and we're called to follow His example. Taking the mindset of Christ, we're commanded to give ourselves up for one another.

Read the following passages and reflect on things you may need to sacrifice and surrender for the cause of Christ.

> The one who loves father or mother more than Me is not worthy of Me; and the one who loves son or daughter more than Me is not worthy of Me. And the one who does not take his cross and follow after Me is not worthy of Me. (Matthew 10:37–38)

_____

_____

_____

_____

> If anyone wants to come after Me, he must deny himself, take up his cross, and follow Me. For whoever wants to save his life will lose it; but whoever loses his life for My sake will find it. (Matthew 16:24–25)

_____

_____

_____

_____

> Do nothing from selfishness or empty conceit, but with humility consider one another as more important than yourselves; do not merely look out for your own personal

interests, but also for the interests of others. (Philippians 2:3–4)

_____

_____

_____

_____

Day 4 Remember and Read

Remember: From *Mission Possible,* page 107:

When we embrace the resistance and consider interruptions in our progress as opportunities, we gain greater strength and endurance. We build up stamina to continue to run the race. This is similar to what happens when we work out. When we exercise our muscles, they get microtears. When we keep exercising consistently, the microtears accumulate to form muscle mass. In a sense, our bodies have to be broken down to come back stronger. The same can be true of our lives. Maybe it's time to start looking at setbacks not as dead ends but as detours to take us to greater destinations.

As you follow along in the *Mission Possible* book, read chapters 8 and 9 this week. Capture any statements or phrases that motivated or challenged you that you'd like to share with the group next week.

_____

_____

_____

_____

_____

A Prayer for You

Father in heaven, thank You for the greatest sacrifice You gave to us, Your Son, and for giving us the free gift of eternal life. I pray for the reader working through this Bible study. You see their heart. You see the picture of their life. If they are overwhelmed by challenges, by fear, by doubt, by lack, may You provide Your power, Your provision, and whatever it is they need to not just get through their challenge but thrive in it. Remind them, Lord, that You are able. And because of that truth, they are able. In Jesus's name. Amen.

Session 5

PURPOSE IN THE PAIN

Mission Vision

Purpose can be found in the most unusual of places. A mission-possible life is lived not only in special moments; it's also lived in the pain-filled ones.

A Quick Look in the Rearview Mirror

Share one thing that stood out to you most from last week's lesson, video, reading, or discussion.

Jump Start

There is nothing neutral about living a mission-possible life. Mission doesn't manifest only in the moments when we see a life changed or the light turned on in the darkness. Living on mission is a constant effort. Psalm 118:24 reminds us that "this is the day which the LORD has made; let's rejoice and be glad in it." In other words, no matter what the day holds, no matter what lies in store for us, let's do our best to crush it. Let's love hard, live well, exercise our faith, pray boldly, run an extra mile, make better decisions, and sacrifice a little more.

We don't wait for an awakening or a special moment in time before pursuing our purpose. We aren't passive about it. Instead, we choose to activate the power of God within us by whatever means are ours—to embrace what He has put before us and use it for His glory. This can mean embracing the hard work of grinding out the responsibilities that come with pursuing a calling. It might look like being committed to the cause of Christ when distractions flood our senses and try to send us running in another direction. Or it might be us praying for others when we feel discouraged that our own prayers are going unnoticed.

It's challenging to live mission possible when life has thrown us curveballs and where we are looks nothing like our best life ever. Sometimes when we've landed in a destination that resembles a barren wasteland, when our best plans have failed, when our health has deteriorated, when our emotional or mental health has suffocated every positive breath out of our bodies, it seems impossible to move mission forward. How can we? We barely have enough steam to crawl out of bed in the morning!

I don't think it's healthy to dismiss our problems as if they don't exist. I mean, none of us has the power to ignore problems away. But we can find ourselves so saddled with stress and the questions that tag along that we get and stay stuck. Stranded in pain and loss and heartache, we want so badly to figure the mess out. *How did I get here? Why did it happen? How can I make it stop?* While I don't know the answer to any of these questions, I do know the perfect solution. His name is Jesus. And if we let Him, He can take that pain, turn it into hope, and use it for good. Yes, even pain can be purposed for good.

When you give it to Him, God will never waste your pain. He will never waste your heartache. He will never waste your loss. When you say yes and live mission possible, God can and will use even the bad to orchestrate good.

Talk About It

Name an instance when short-term pain brought about a positive long-term result.

Video Teaching

Watch video session 5. While viewing the video, use the outline and spaces below to record key ideas or any thoughts you want to remember.

➢ _____

_____

➢ _____

_____

➢ _____

_____

➢ _____

_____

➢ _____

_____

➢ _____

_____

➤ _____

_____

Mission-Driven Discussion

1. In the video teaching, we learned that the reason we can endure through pain is because Christ ultimately endured for us on the cross. He didn't retreat. He didn't back down. He stood firm, kept His convictions, and suffered for our sake. That's love, folks. Describe a time in your life you had the opportunity to show love in a painful situation.

_____

_____

_____

_____

2. In the video teaching, I talk about my friends Jeff and Becky Davidson. Becky stood by her husband, Jeff, through the thick and thin, to the end. She writes, "Had I not done the hard things, had I cut bait and run, I would have more regrets now than I think I could bear." Becky knew that there was purpose in her pain and that's why she could endure. She trusted God would use their story to impact lives. And He has. How does Becky's faith encourage you to live?

_____

_____

_____

_____

3. Talk about someone in your life who, despite some type of limitation or difficulty, is a living testament of consistency, passion, joy, and grace in shining the light of Jesus in this world of darkness. What do you think is his or her motivation? How has this person's example influenced who you are?

_____

_____

_____

_____

4. Read 2 Corinthians 12:7–10:

Because of the extraordinary greatness of the revelations, for this reason, to keep me from exalting myself, there was given to me a thorn in the flesh, a messenger of Satan to torment me—to keep me from exalting myself! Concerning this I pleaded with the Lord three times that it might leave me. And He has said to me, "My grace is sufficient for you, for power is perfected in weakness." Most gladly, therefore, I will rather boast about my weaknesses, so that the power of Christ may dwell in me. Therefore I delight in weaknesses, in insults, in distresses, in persecutions, in difficulties, in behalf of Christ; for when I am weak, then I am strong.

Although Paul didn't shy away from mentioning the "thorn in the flesh" (verse 7) he wrestled with, we don't know what his specific problem was. According to this passage, what negative effect did it have on him?

_____

_____

_____

_____

5. The *Mission Possible* book highlights the importance of being all in, being committed to a mission-driven life, particularly when it gets hard and the temptation to quit poses a great threat. From page 142:

We never give up our mission to love God and others. We never quit serving God and others. We don't quit praying for our loved ones' freedom from addiction, for their salvation, for their healing, for their wholeness. We don't stop studying, practicing, and preparing.

Name a time when your commitment to what God has called you to do was threatened because the stress became too great. What was the outcome? Looking back, what could you have done differently?

_____

_____

_____

_____

6. How has physical suffering affected your relationship with God?

_____

_____

_____

_____

7. The *Mission Possible* book, page 143, teaches about living with the right kind of intensity: "You have to live with open eyes to see the needs, an open heart to love, and open hands to serve." How would you say your life, right now, reflects this statement? How true, or challenging, is this when you are experiencing pain, loss, or a problem?

_____

_____

_____

_____

Send-Off and Group Prayer

Today we have learned that there is always a purpose, even in pain. God is not absent. He has not forsaken you and never will. Your suffering is not in vain. I promise you that if you let Him, He will use it for the greater good.

Let's close our time together in prayer. Here are some ideas from this session that can guide your conversation with God:

- Ask Him to reveal areas in your life that may keep you from being fully united with Him.
- Thank Him that His love is faithful and never changes no matter how you feel.
- Ask Him to help you open your eyes and heart to be aware of and meet the needs of others.
- Pray for opportunities in which you can use your hard places for purpose.

Your Midweek Mission:
Four Days of Exercises and Prayer to Go Deeper

Day 1 Study and Reflect

Jesus meets us in our pain. It is in suffering that the Cross invites us to fellowship and in the Resurrection that our suffering finds hope. Theologian Jürgen Moltmann wrote, "When we feel pain we participate in his pain, and when we grieve we share his grief. . . . People who believe in the God who suffers with us, recognize their suffering in God, and God in their suffering."[15]

God sent His own Son, Jesus Christ, to this earth to die a terrible death in our place so we would not have to be punished for our sins. He did this out of His great love for us. Suffering starts with Jesus, but it doesn't stop there. We continue to carry the cross in following His example as His followers. First Peter 2:20 says, "What credit is there if, when you sin and are harshly treated, you endure it with patience? But if when you do what is right and suffer for it you patiently endure it, this finds favor with God."

Yet here's the thing. We don't suffer without a purpose. We don't suffer so God can get some twisted satisfaction out of it or so we can "see how it feels."

Read the following scriptures. Then reflect on the value of suffering on the life of a believer, and write down how each passage motivates you to continue to live mission possible.

We do not lose heart, but though our outer person is decaying, yet our inner person is being renewed day by day. For our momentary, light affliction is producing for us an eternal weight of glory far beyond all comparison, while we look not at the things which are seen, but at the things which are not seen; for the things which are seen are temporal, but the things which are not seen are eternal. (2 Corinthians 4:16–18)

_____

_____

_____

_____

Consider it all joy, my brothers and sisters, when you encounter various trials, knowing that the testing of your faith produces endurance. And let endurance have its perfect result, so that you may be perfect and complete, lacking in nothing. (James 1:2–4)

_____

_____

In this you greatly rejoice, even though now for a little while, if necessary, you have been distressed by various trials, so that the proof of your faith, being more precious than gold which perishes though tested by fire, may be found to result in praise, glory, and honor at the revelation of Jesus Christ. (1 Peter 1:6–7)

Horatio Spafford had a loving wife and five adorable children and made a substantial living as a lawyer. He was a pillar in his Chicago community. The early 1870s turned out to be horrible for him and his family.[16] His four-year-old son died of scarlet fever, and as he and his wife were nursing their tender wounds, just a short while later the Great Fire of Chicago destroyed practically everything they owned. A religious man, Horatio kept his faith and did the best he could to make the most of his life in light of those two terrible events. Two years later, in November 1873, the family took a trip to Europe to catch their breath. Horatio sent his wife and four girls ahead of him, as he needed to tie up a number of loose ends concerning his business. He waved goodbye to his family and watched as the ship sailed off. He would meet up with them in England in a week or so. Soon, Horatio received a cable from his wife. It read, "Saved alone."[17]

The ship that had carried his wife and four daughters had been struck by another vessel and, in only a few minutes, sank deep into the ocean. Two hundred twenty-six people lost their lives in that accident, including Horatio's young girls.

A few days after hearing of the death of all his daughters, Horatio left Chicago and took off for England on a ship to meet his wife. I cannot even imagine how slow time must have crawled as the ship sailed across the Atlantic. What was he thinking? Was he angry? Was he tempted to give up?

At one point during Horatio's journey, the captain of the ship, knowing about Horatio's recent loss, beckoned for him to come on deck. As the waves gently slapped the sides of the ship, the captain grimly pointed out a particular spot in the swirling blue sea that glistened like sapphire diamonds. It was where Horatio's daughters had drowned. I imagine hot tears stung his cheeks as his heart sank to the ocean floor. Four girls, flesh of his flesh, dead in an instant. What Horatio did next is nothing less than a true act of faith and worship. He took out a pen and started scribbling some notes—something about a quiet assurance, a buoyant trust in God even in spite of His seeming absence and events that simply should not have been:

> When peace, like a river, attendeth my way,
> When sorrows like sea billows roll;
> Whatever my lot, Thou hast taught me to know,
> It is well, it is well with my soul.[18]

Horatio could have forgotten God. He could have cursed the One who had the power to walk on water and calm angry seas. He could have drowned in his own bitter waters. But through the unexplained tragedies, the blinding tears, and the bottomless sorrow, he wanted to make known that it was well with his soul.

I want to invite you to write a poem, song, or letter to God expressing your heartfelt thoughts on His presence, His character, His faithfulness, and His love in a season (present or past) in which you have experienced great pain. Ask Him to reveal to you how purpose has been woven into the pain.

_____

_____

_____

_____

_____

_____

Day 2 Review, Reflect, and Remember

Review chapters 8 and 9 in *Mission Possible*.

Reflect: Write down what you learned, a breakthrough you experienced, or a shift in perspective you gained from this lesson, the book, the video, or discussions. Prepare to share with the group next week.

_____

_____

_____

_____

What scripture spoke to you most this week? Try to memorize it. Write it down and then put it someplace where you'll see it when you spend some time alone each day; for example, on the bathroom mirror, your car dashboard, or your laptop cover.

_____

_____

_____

_____

Remember: From *Mission Possible,* page 142:

When you are committed to a mission, nothing can stop you. You live with a heightened sense of awareness, particularly of your purpose. You have a vision of who you are and who God created you to be. You understand that your time on earth is limited and live with an underlying sense of urgency. You focus on what you need to do now and what you need to do next.

Day 3 Study and Reflect

The peace of God, which transcends all human understanding, fuels mission-possible living. Embracing this divine peace allows faith warriors to continue to fight and live with purpose despite pain, suffering, and uncertainty. When you know the security God provides, you attack life with holy confidence, sharing with others how they, too, can experience it.

Today I'd like you to reflect on and write out your story (specifically what God has done in your life). I believe a person's story is a powerful and effective evangelism tool. You might be thinking that your story is boring or irrelevant or that you don't have an outrageous testimony. That's a lie from the Evil One. You are one of a kind. Out of the more than 7.5 billion people living on this earth, your experiences are unique to just you. No one in history—past, present, or future—has lived or will ever live your life. That's pretty significant. Skeptics may be able to dismiss a well-thought-out apologetic argument or a pastor's sermon on Sunday morning, but they cannot discredit your own personal testimony.

While living under persecution, Peter gave his brothers and sisters from Asia Minor these instructions: "Sanctify Christ as Lord in your hearts, always being ready to make a defense to everyone who asks you to give an account for the hope that is in you, but with gentleness and respect" (1 Peter 3:15). If someone today walked up and asked you why you believe what you believe, would you have an answer? Would you be able to give an account for the hope that is in you?

In the New Testament, on multiple occasions, the apostle Paul shared his testimony as an on-ramp for gospel conversations. In one specific incident, he stood boldly before King Herod Agrippa II and very simply made a case for Christ based on his conversion experience and commission. Luke recorded this account in Acts 26:1–23. Read the passage and answer the questions that follow it.

Agrippa said to Paul, "You are permitted to speak for yourself." Then Paul extended his hand and proceeded to make his defense:

"Regarding all the things of which I am accused by the Jews, King Agrippa, I consider myself fortunate that I am about to make my defense before you today, especially because you are an expert in all customs and questions among the Jews; therefore I beg you to listen to me patiently.

"So then, all Jews know my way of life since my youth, which from the beginning was spent among my own nation and in Jerusalem, since they have known about me for a long time, if they are willing to testify, that I lived as a Pharisee according to the strictest sect of our religion. And now I am standing trial for the hope of the promise made by God to our fathers; the promise to which our twelve tribes hope to attain, as they earnestly serve God night and day. For this hope, O king, I am being accused by Jews. Why is it considered incredible among you people if God raises the dead?

"So I thought to myself that I had to act in strong opposition to the name of Jesus of Nazareth. And this is just what I did in Jerusalem; not only did I lock up many of the saints in prisons, after receiving authority from the chief priests, but I also cast my vote against them when they were being put to death. And as I punished them often in all the synagogues, I tried to force them to blaspheme; and since I was extremely enraged at them, I kept pursuing them even to foreign cities.

"While so engaged, as I was journeying to Damascus with the authority and commission of the chief priests, at midday, O king, I saw on the way a light from heaven, brighter than the sun, shining around me and those who were journeying with me. And when we had all fallen to the ground, I heard a voice saying to me in the Hebrew dialect, 'Saul, Saul, why are you persecuting Me? It is hard for you to kick against the goads.' And I said, 'Who are You, Lord?' And the Lord said, 'I am Jesus whom you are persecuting. But get up and stand on your feet; for this purpose I have appeared to you, to appoint you as a servant and a witness not only to the things in which you have seen Me, but also to the things in which I will appear to you, rescuing you from the Jewish people and from the Gentiles, to whom I am sending you, to open their eyes so that they may turn from darkness to light, and from the power of Satan to God, that they may receive forgiveness of sins and an inheritance among those who have been sanctified by faith in Me.'

"For that reason, King Agrippa, I did not prove disobedient to the heavenly vision, but continually proclaimed to those in Damascus first, and in Jerusalem, and then all the region of Judea, and even to the Gentiles, that they are to repent and turn to God, performing deeds consistent with repentance. For these reasons some Jews seized me in the temple and tried to murder me. So, having obtained help from God, I stand to this day testifying both to small and great, stating nothing but what the Prophets and Moses said was going to take place, as to whether the Christ was to suffer, and whether, as first from the resurrection of the dead, He would proclaim light both to the Jewish people and to the Gentiles."

What was Paul's life like before he encountered Jesus on the road to Damascus?

_____

_____

_____

_____

Describe Paul's conversion experience.

_____

_____

_____

_____

What was Paul's life like after he encountered Jesus? What was his new mission?

_____

_____

_____

_____

Now it's your turn! Just like Paul, we, too, must be ready and able to share when asked. If you've never written out your story before, it's okay. Most people haven't. I want to help you do that. Here's a simple exercise to get your mind thinking about your lifesaving relationship with Jesus Christ. Grab your phone and pull up the clock app. Set a timer for three minutes per question. When the time is up, reset the timer and move on to the next question. You can always go back and add more detail later.

Ready, set, go!

What was your life like before Christ? Describe your attitude, habits, relationships, and so on.

_____

_____

_____

_____

What caused you to consider Jesus?

_____

_____

_____

_____

How and when did you choose to follow Him? Or if you have not made that decision yet, what keeps you from following Him?

_____

_____

_____

How has your life changed since making that decision? How is your life different now? List some specific changes in your character, attitude, and habits.

_____

_____

_____

How do you see God using you now and in the future?

_____

_____

_____

_____

What are some ways that you think God wants to use you but that you haven't said yes to yet?

_____

_____

_____

_____

Great job! Now that you've taken some time to jot down your initial thoughts, use the space below to consolidate the answers you just gave. In two or three paragraphs, write out what your life was like before Jesus, what happened when you experienced Him, and what your life looks like now because of Him.

_____

_____

_____

_____

_____

_____

_____

As we develop a mission-possible mindset, it is worth noting that Paul did not merely share his subjective, personal experience; he wove together in his story the more objective, universal gospel story that must be proclaimed to all people. Paul crafted a dual-themed masterpiece that spoke of his unique encounter with Jesus and the sacrificial-love message of God's story. As we consider sharing our testimonies, we should, like Paul, weave together a twofold story that combines our individual experience with the love that God offers through the Cross.

Day 4 Remember and Read

Remember: From *Mission Possible,* page 146:

As you wait for wisdom, an answer to prayer, or even healing, if you allow Him to, God will always position you to be used for His glory. Purpose is always present, even in the waiting.

If you are following along in the *Mission Possible* book, read chapter 10 this week. Capture any statements or phrases that motivated or challenged you that you'd like to share with the group next week.

_____

_____

_____

_____

A Prayer for You

Lord God, I pray that You would draw near this reader. If they are tired or weak or if life feels impossible, remind them that You are right by their side and that You will be faithful to complete what You have started in their life. Use their pain to transform the lives of others. Create in them an open and ready heart, willing to be used at any moment and even in difficult times to bring help and healing to others. In Jesus's name I pray. Amen.

Session 6

MISSION ETERNAL

Mission Vision

Your life counts because of whose you are, so use what you have wherever you are, and make each day bigger than just yourself.

A Quick Look in the Rearview Mirror

Share one thing that stood out to you most from last week's lesson, video, reading, or discussion.

Jump Start

One area of my life in which I feel I've been really humbled is marriage. Having the honor of being Demi's husband has given me an inside look at how sinful and selfish I can be! It's given me an opportunity to serve and grow like no other experience in my life. It's beautiful to have someone by your side for the rest of your life. It's also an opportunity to step outside your comfort zone to choose to serve someone else. I'm sure Jesus wasn't comfortable when He was on the cross, but He wasn't focused on Himself. He understood His mission and was willing to lay down His life because of the love He has for us.

I am so grateful that God offered Jesus, His only Son, to die for our sins so that we may have eternal life. What does this sacrifice mean for us? I love how the Bible puts it: "This is eternal life, that they may know You, the only true God, and Jesus Christ whom You have sent" (John 17:3). I want to invest in eternity, and because people last forever, I want to invest in them. More than anything, I want to leave a legacy of having influenced others for good and, most importantly, for Jesus. As believers, we are not called to merely survive life, although at times that's pretty much how it feels. We are called to thrive—to, as Jesus put it, live abundant lives (see John 10:10), looking not to satisfy our own needs and preferences but to influence others for eternity.

When I began, as a young boy, to realize that heaven—not the farmhouse my parents owned in Jacksonville—is my home, my perspective on how I lived each day began to change. I realized that my time on earth ought not to be spent just occupying space or resting without aim. Although we are on earth partly to glorify God, we also have a job to do. Whether you call it the Great Commission or any other name, our mission is to love God and love people. And we are called to do that in our own unique way.

Don't let the Enemy trick you into believing that your life won't matter because you are not a celebrity or influencer or don't have a million followers. You are a divine masterpiece created to do great things—great things that can have an eternal impact.

While you can't save someone in your own power, you might be able to plant a seed to inspire hope. You can share the gospel with someone. You can lead a person to a place in his heart where he will be open to Jesus. You can encourage someone with a kind word. You can brighten a person's day in her darkest hour of need. Where that seed goes and how it grows is up to God.

The power of the gospel stems from the greatest trade in the history of the world: humanity's sin for the righteousness of Jesus

Christ, God's only Son. It's a message we can't help but share. It's called good news for a reason. Why would we want to keep it to ourselves? Let's live mission possible and keep pushing the mission forward into a future that lasts forever.

Talk About It

How does the idea of having eternal life through Jesus inform the decisions you make each day?

Video Teaching

Watch video session 6. While viewing the video, use the outline and spaces below to record key ideas or any thoughts you want to remember.

➢ _____

_____

➢ _____

_____

➢ _____

_____

➢ _____

_____

➢ _____

➤ _____

_____

_____

Mission-Driven Discussion

1. In the video teaching, I shared that mission-possible living is about running for eternal things—heavenly rewards that last forever (1 Corinthians 9:24–27). However, most of the time we tend to pursue what's temporary; that is, pleasure, money, medals, trophies, and so on. Paul calls those things crowns that will not last or "perishable wreath[s]." As you reflect on your life, what is something you have chased that wasn't worth it?

_____

_____

_____

_____

2. In the video teaching, I also share a quote from one of my favorite movies, *Gladiator*. In the movie, the main character, Maximus Decimus Meridius, says, "What we do in life echoes in eternity." I believe he has it right. What do you want your echo to be? How do you want to be remembered?

_____

_____

_____

_____

3. Name three ways in which you can make your life count.

_____

_____

_____

_____

4. Read 2 Timothy 4:7–8:

> I have fought the good fight, I have finished the course, I have kept the faith; in the future there is reserved for me the crown of righteousness, which the Lord, the righteous Judge, will award to me on that day; and not only to me, but also to all who have loved His appearing.

This second epistle was the last one written by Paul to his ministry partner Timothy. Paul was in jail at the time, and it wouldn't be long before he would be executed for his faith. Despite the sad reality of his impending death, Paul was positive in his letter to Timothy. It was great encouragement to his co-laborer, and to us today, to fight the good fight of faith and run well the race set before us.

Mission Possible Bible Study

Is there anything you need to change about how you live each day on earth so that you are able to share Paul's sentiment in 2 Timothy 4:7–8?

_____

_____

_____

_____

5. How often do you think about what you go through on earth in light of heaven? How does the thought of living with Jesus for eternity bring you comfort or peace? What are you most looking forward to when you get to heaven?

_____

_____

_____

_____

6. How do you define a life well lived? How does your definition differ from the perspective a nonbeliever might have?

_____

_____

_____

_____

7. Read Ephesians 5:15–17:

> Be very careful, then, how you live—not as unwise but as wise, making the most of every opportunity, because the days are evil. Therefore do not be foolish, but understand what the Lord's will is. (NIV)

Does this passage motivate you to align your priorities with what really matters? What opportunities do you need to make the most of?

_____

_____

_____

_____

8. From *Mission Possible,* page 176:

> We can't get too comfortable with life on earth. We won't be here forever. What matters more than the fun we have or the stuff we accumulate is what we did with the time we were given. The Bible tells us, "If you have been raised with Christ, keep seeking the things that are above, where Christ is, seated at the right hand of God. Set your minds on the things that are above, not on the things that are on earth" (Colossians 3:1–2).
>
> Instead of seeking success in our own lives, we seek to bring faith, hope, and love to those needing a brighter day in their darkest hour of need. That's not just our foundation's mission statement; that's our hearts' cry. I don't know what your mission is, but I hope it's one that makes your heart long for Jesus and love people.

As we near the end of this Bible study, have you given any thought to your mission statement? What do you think it might be? Take turns sharing it with the group, or write it down in the space below.

_____

_____

_____

_____

_____

_____

Send-Off and Group Prayer

In this session, we have learned that as we live mission possible, we live knowing that this earth is not our home. One day we will live with Jesus in heaven for all eternity. So as we have breath on this earth, may we craft lives of significance and make decisions that lean into God's best.

Let's close in prayer. Here are some ideas from this session that can guide your conversation with God:

- Thank Him that this world isn't all there is.
- Ask Him for continued opportunities to make your life count.
- Pray for the strength and courage to live each day with an eternal perspective, knowing that the darkness will not last forever.
- Thank God for the hope of heaven, which promises an eternal life beyond the messy and dark world we live in.

Your Midweek Mission:
Four Days of Exercises and Prayer to Go Deeper

Day 1 Study and Reflect

Our view of eternity shapes how we live each day on earth. As believers, we ought to have a different perspective than others do. Our outlook on life is anchored in hope because we have received the gift of eternal life. Not only that, but how we choose to invest our time, talents, and resources will be based not on what is temporary but on what is eternal. Everything looks different from an eternal perspective.

How are you living today in light of eternity? Write down two examples. How does having an eternal mindset encourage or strengthen your character and faith in your daily life?

_____

_____

_____

_____

Read 1 Peter 4:7–11:

The end of all things is near; therefore, be of sound judgment and sober spirit for the purpose of prayer. Above all, keep fervent in your love for one another, because love covers a multitude of sins. Be hospitable to one another without complaint. As each one has received a special gift, employ it in serving one another as good stewards of the multifaceted grace of God. Whoever speaks is to do so as one who is speaking actual words of God; whoever serves is to do so as one who is serving by the strength which God supplies; so that in all things God may be glorified through Jesus Christ, to whom belongs the glory and dominion for-ever and ever. Amen.

What are three practical directives offered in this passage that can help you guide how you live and what choices you make?

_____

_____

_____

_____

Living in the moment can be a positive approach in many circum-stances. After all, it's great to be present and fully enjoy where you are and what you are doing and with whom. However, some people would say part of this means following your heart in a "you only live once" kind of way: doing what you feel like doing in the moment. But that's not necessarily always the right thing to do. Being fully present with your loved ones in the moment or focusing on a task at hand while ignoring unhelpful distractions are actions that should be encouraged. In the same vein, as believers, we shouldn't always do what we feel like doing in a particular moment. Deciding on a whim to cash in your savings to spend a week on a Caribbean island might not be the best choice you can make.

We want to be wise in how we use our gifts to contribute to God's work. We want to live in a way that encourages and serves others. We want to leave behind a lasting mark on this world. We want to live with the big picture in mind, a long view, not immediately satisfy what we long for or crave or feel like doing if it doesn't align with God's best.

Read 1 Corinthians 3:12–15:

If anyone builds on the foundation with gold, silver, precious stones, wood, hay, or straw, each one's work will become evident; for the day will show it because it is to be revealed with fire, and the fire itself will test the quality of each one's work. If anyone's work which he has built on it remains, he will receive a reward. If anyone's work is burned up, he will suffer loss; but he himself will be saved, yet only so as through fire.

Think about the past seventy-two hours. What choices did you make that satisfied your momentary pleasure instead of invested in your personal or spiritual growth? What choices strengthened your faith life and eternal perspective?

_____

_____

_____

_____

Day 2 Review, Reflect, and Remember

Review chapter 10 in *Mission Possible*.

Reflect: Write down what you learned, a breakthrough you experienced, or a shift in perspective you gained from this lesson, the book, the video, or discussions. Prepare to share with the group next week.

_____

_____

_____

_____

What scripture spoke to you most this week? Try to memorize it. Write it down and then put it someplace where you'll see it when you spend some time alone each day; for example, on the bathroom mirror, your car dashboard, or your laptop cover.

_____

_____

_____

_____

Remember: From *Mission Possible,* pages 165–66:

The world defines success in many different ways. Maybe it's accumulating a certain number of followers on social media, gaining public recognition for an accomplishment, or crossing off the checklist you created when you graduated from college. I hope you reach your goals and get the gold star or hold the trophy up high. But there's something limiting about success as defined by the world. It's self-oriented. . . . Significance, however, is about others, loving and serving people. One of the greatest questions you can ask yourself is, *Does my life change other people's lives for the better?*

When you're focused on others—when your priorities are wrapped around the Great Commission, bringing the love of Jesus to hurting people—your life counts for more than a title people will forget or an achievement someone will probably surpass in time. Years ago, I heard it said that one of the greatest tragedies in life is to look back one day and say, "I was successful in things that don't matter."

Day 3 Study and Reflect

In session 2, I mentioned that the book of Ecclesiastes is a tough but insightful piece of wisdom literature. In it, the wise King Solomon offers us key pieces of timeless truth in his attempt to find meaning in various pursuits. Though the tone of the book may sound pessimistic at times, its basic goal is to provide clarity on what matters most.

In Ecclesiastes 3:11, Solomon wrote,

He has made everything appropriate in its time. He has also set eternity in their heart, without the possibility that mankind will find out the work which God has done from the beginning even to the end.

Over the centuries, there has been considerable difficulty and disagreement over the precise meaning of this passage. However, from what we can observe, Solomon made three major conclusions:

1. God has made everything appropriate in its time.
2. God has set eternity in the human heart.
3. We cannot fully understand God's eternal work.

Read Ecclesiastes 3:1–8 for broader context:

There is an appointed time for everything. And there is a time for every matter under heaven—

A time to give birth and a time to die;
A time to plant and a time to uproot what is planted.

A time to kill and a time to heal;
A time to tear down and a time to build up.
A time to weep and a time to laugh;
A time to mourn and a time to dance.
A time to throw stones and a time to gather stones;
A time to embrace and a time to shun embracing.
A time to search and a time to give up as lost;
A time to keep and a time to throw away.
A time to tear apart and a time to sew together;
A time to be silent and a time to speak.
A time to love and a time to hate;
A time for war and a time for peace.

What is the major theme? How does this passage shape your conception of time?

_____

_____

_____

_____

Let's go back and do a deep dive into the three conclusions Solomon makes in Ecclesiastes 3:11.

1. God Has Made Everything Appropriate in Its Time

In God's perfect, absolute, and complete knowledge, "there is an appointed time for everything" (verse 1). And in this appointed time, He has made everything appropriate, or beautiful. Solomon challenges readers to see time from a divine context, not a human one. From God's eternal perspective, every event, season, occurrence, and experience is created order. What you and I perceive as a mystery, God sees as prearranged and part of His plan. From eternity past to eternity future, God's timing is always working for His purposes. Toward the end of his life, King Solomon finally realized this truth: "Everything God does will remain forever; there is nothing to add to it and there is nothing to take from it" (verse 14).

You often hear people say "Everything happens for a reason." When offered flippantly or without sincere care for human suffering, it can become a cliché statement used to try to make sense of our circumstances. But poor execution doesn't negate the very true reality that God is sovereign. We don't always get to know the *why* behind things that happen, but just like Solomon, we can find hope in knowing that no matter what occurs in our lives or this world, God is at work for our ultimate good.

How have you seen the timeliness of God in your life?

_____

_____

_____

2. God Has Set Eternity in the Human Heart

It is no surprise that Solomon recognized the fact that God has set eternity in our hearts. After not denying himself any pleasure, possessions, and power, he was ultimately left unsatisfied (see 2:1–11). There was still something more he desired. In every human soul, there is an innate hunger for something we cannot see. There is a God-given desire for eternity hardwired into our very nature. Being created in the likeness of an eternal being, we yearn for what is to come.

Bible teacher Mike Mazzalongo noted,

All the parts of life, when put together, do not equal something meaningful. To have meaning you have to add the part or Person who is outside of time. Our yearning for eternity and eternal life can only be satisfied by discovering the person, the work and the salvation found in Jesus Christ. This is why Jesus says that He is yesterday, today and tomorrow: We only understand eternity and its meaning when we accept Christ, who is both the author of time and beyond time (Colossians 1:15–17).[19]

What longings do you have that never seem to be fulfilled? What do your longings mean in light of eternity?

_____

_____

_____

3. We Cannot Fully Understand God's Eternal Work

A simple fact in life is that He is God and we are not. As God moves forward toward final restoration in Christ, we're left waiting in anticipation. Our knowledge is limited; we will never fully discover God's complete work. Although we yearn for paradise to come, we find hope in God's story. From the creation (see Genesis 1–2) to the original sin (see Genesis 3) to redemption in Jesus (see Romans 3:21–31) to a new heaven and new earth (see Revelation 21:1), we must humble ourselves and fix our eyes on the future celebration—that is, a never-ending party in heaven with our Lord!

How does Ecclesiastes 3:11 teach you to live with a sense of urgency?

_____

_____

_____

In living mission eternal, we don't just sit around waiting for God to wrap everything up someday. In Matthew 28:19–20, Jesus instructed His disciples to "*go*, therefore, and make disciples of all the nations, baptizing them in the name of the Father and the Son and the Holy Spirit, teaching them to follow all that I commanded you." That same calling and responsibility falls on our shoulders.

Understanding we won't have it all figured out, Peter encouraged us to "grow in the grace and knowledge of our Lord and Savior Jesus Christ" (2 Peter 3:18).

In Philippians 3:13–14, Paul asserted, "I do not regard myself as having taken hold of it yet; but one thing I do: forgetting what lies behind and reaching forward to what lies ahead, I press on toward the goal for the prize of the upward call of God in Christ Jesus."

What was Paul's ultimate goal? What can you begin to do to adopt a mission-eternal mindset this week?

_____

_____

_____

Day 4 Remember and Reflect

Remember: From *Mission Possible*, page 167:

Every single one of us has a chance to make a difference. We have the opportunity, the ability, and the capacity to do something to build the kingdom of God. It's not because we're great or qualified or successful; it's mission possible because we've teamed up with the God of this universe. When we take aim into the future and live lives of significance, anything is possible.

As you complete this study, think about and write down three ways this teaching has informed your faith and encouraged you to lean into God, knowing that making an eternal difference is mission possible.

_____

_____

_____

_____

_____

_____

A Prayer for You

Dear Lord, remind the reader of this Bible study that You have created them for a purpose—for a reason that is significant and far outlasts earthly success. Create and nurture in them a mindset that is focused not on the things of this world but on that which is eternal. Surround them with strength to live in Your hope. In Jesus's name. Amen.

A FINAL WORD

Thank you so much for joining me and working through this Bible study. My prayer is that you turn this final page feeling excited about the days ahead.

As you begin or continue to live mission possible, focus on these takeaways:

- Execute the good works that God has already prepared for you to do.
- Do what lies before you wholeheartedly, with purpose and intention.
- Trust God with the plan even though you might not see each and every step before you take it.
- Push through the resistance with the end goal in sight.
- Find purpose in all things, even pain-filled moments.
- Make each day bigger than just yourself.

I am proud of you for believing in your mission. I'm rooting for you.

Let's go live it out!

NOTES

1. Robert L. Thomas, *New American Standard Exhaustive Concordance of the Bible: Hebrew-Aramaic and Greek Dictionaries*, rev. ed. (Anaheim, CA: Foundation, 1998), https://biblehub.com/greek/4161.htm.

2. Thomas R. W. Longstaff, "Holy Spirit," in Mark Allan Powell, ed., *HarperCollins Bible Dictionary*, rev. ed. (New York: HarperCollins, 2011), 386–87.

3. Thomas, *New American Standard*, https://biblehub.com/greek/3875.htm.

4. Max Anders, *Holman New Testament Commentary*, vol. 8, *Galatians, Ephesians, and Colossians* (Nashville: Broadman, Holman, 1999), 172.

5. Francis Brown et al., *The NAS Old Testament Hebrew Lexicon*, Strong's Number 1892, s.v. "*hebel*," www.biblestudytools.com/lexicons/hebrew/nas/hebel.html.

6. Travis Bean, "All 24 Marvel Cinematic Universe Films Ranked at the Box Office—Including 'Black Widow,'" *Forbes*, April 24, 2020, www.forbes.com/sites/travisbean/2020/04/24/all-23-marvel-cinematic-universe-films-ranked-at-the-box-office-including-black-widow/?sh=63ddaa5494e5.

7. *Merriam-Webster*, s.v. "passion (*n.*)," www.merriam-webster.com/dictionary/passion.

8. Thomas, *New American Standard*, https://biblehub.com/greek/3958.htm.

9. *Oxford English Dictionary*, s.v. "compassion (*n.*)," www.oed.com/viewdictionaryentry/Entry/37475.

10. Thomas, *New American Standard,* https://biblehub.com/greek/2072.htm.

11. Leon Morris, *1 Corinthians: An Introduction and Commentary,* vol. 7, Tyndale New Testament Commentaries (Downers Grove, IL: InterVarsity, 1985), 180.

12. Thomas, *New American Standard,* https://biblehub.com/greek/4043.htm.

13. Thomas, *New American Standard,* https://biblehub.com/greek/1491.htm.

14. *Online Etymology Dictionary,* s.v. "sacrifice (*n.*)," www.etymonline.com/word/sacrifice.

15. Jürgen Moltmann, *Jesus Christ for Today's World* (Minneapolis: Fortress, 1994), 45–46.

16. "Saved Alone," American Colony in Jerusalem, 1870 to 2006, Library of Congress, www.loc.gov/collections/american-colony-in-jerusalem/articles-and-essays/a-community-in-jerusalem/saved-alone/; "Horatio Gates Spafford—The Story Behind the Hymn 'It Is Well with My Soul,'" Famous Song Writers, Bethel Church Ripon, December 12, 2018, www.bethelripon.com/life-stories/horatio-gates-spafford.

17. "Telegram from Anna Spafford to Horatio Gates Spafford Re Being 'Saved Alone' Among Her Traveling Party in the Shipwreck of the Ville du Havre," Library of Congress, December 1873, www.loc.gov/item/mamcol000006.

18. Horatio Spafford, "It Is Well with My Soul," 1873, public domain.

19. Mike Mazzalongo, "A Time for Everything, Part 1, Ecclesiastes 3:1–11," BibleTalk.tv, January 2017, https://bibletalk.tv/ecclesiastes-part-4.

TIM TEBOW is a two-time national champion, Heisman Trophy winner, first-round NFL draft pick, and former professional baseball player. Tebow currently serves as a speaker, is a college football analyst with ESPN and the SEC Network, and is the author of four *New York Times* bestsellers, including *Shaken, This Is the Day,* and the children's book *Bronco and Friends: A Party to Remember.* He is the founder and leader of the Tim Tebow Foundation (TTF), whose mission is to bring faith, hope, and love to those needing a brighter day in their darkest hour of need. Tim is married to Demi-Leigh Tebow (née Nel-Peters), a speaker, influencer, entrepreneur, and Miss Universe 2017. Tim and Demi live in Jacksonville, Florida, with their three dogs, Chunk, Kobe, and Paris.

www.timtebow.com
Facebook, Instagram, Twitter: @timtebow
LinkedIn: www.linkedin.com/in/timtebow15
TikTok: @timtebow_15

ALSO AVAILABLE!

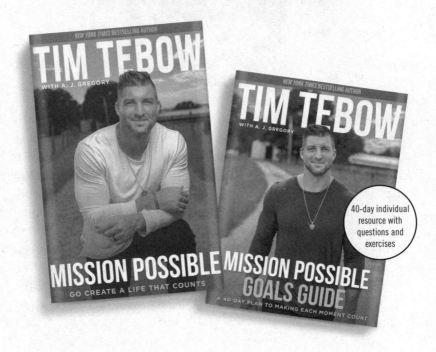